Thirty One
Days of
Victory

Scott Reece

FOREWORD

It is a true honor to write this foreword. I have known Scott for 30 years, first as his Bible college professor, then watching him grow into an exceptional spiritual leader. Scott has a huge mantle, a bigger heart, and very broad shoulders. As you can tell, I believe he is the complete package.

I realize, however, that you're looking for more than strength and character in an author—very important traits, to be sure—but you expect the writer to provide helpful content packaged with readability. As a diligent student, I have studied some great "content books" that, unfortunately, read like a boring encyclopedia. The information contained was valuable, but wading through them was torture. Other books in my library were pleasurable and readable—entertaining, even emotionally gripping—but when finished, I had added nothing to my "winning and overcoming in life" arsenal. It is always refreshing when I find a great content book that is also an enjoyable read. I'm sure you've already guessed where I stand on this one, and you're right. Filled with relevant and helpful information, *Thirty One Days of Victory* is also a page-turner.

As any quick-read, chapter-a-day book must, Scott gets immediately to the point—quickly, yet clearly. Each bite-sized but meaty chapter is short enough to read over your morning coffee. I'm certainly not suggesting you rush through the material; you'll want to think your way through the daily portions, perhaps even revisit the nuggets of truth throughout the day in order to work them into your soul. I'm simply assuring you that while substantive, Scott spares us the unnecessary preachy fluff.

Then, and perhaps most importantly, there is the fact that in *Thirty One Days of Victory*, Scott Reece is writing what he has lived. Many authors and preachers elaborate on subjects they understand from their studies; depending on the subject matter, this is okay, perhaps even commendable. But as you know, nothing empowers a message as much as the messenger having lived it. Head knowledge can be taught. Only heart knowledge, however, worked into our spirit as we *experience* a truth, can be imparted.

Scott has had to live the victory message he preaches. When his first wife, Veronica, passed away unexpectedly and very suddenly, leaving him to mourn and carry on as a single parent and pastor, his choices were to overcome or quit. Some trials simply leave no middle ground. Personally, I cannot imagine a greater crisis of faith. But from a reservoir deep within, Scott found strength to claw, crawl, and stumble forward. Eventually, he found his stride once again. The process proved him, deepened him, and seasoned him. And we get to eat the fruit.

I promise you: read, think, meditate, and pray your way through this book over 31 days, and you'll be different. The scriptures tell us our journey in life must be one of going from faith to faith and strength to strength (Romans 1:17; Psalms 84:7). This book is your next step in that process. It will make you stronger, wiser, and more equipped to live the life of an overcomer. Then, and I'm quite certain of this, you'll want to order Scott's first two books: *Thirty One Days of Healing* and *Thirty One Days of Peace*.

Get ready to be inspired.

Dr. Dutch Sheets
Best-selling author

DEDICATION

In each of our lives, we are the results of the investments that many others have made into us. Throughout my life, I am blessed to have had so many people pour their hearts and lives into who I am. I have been the recipient of the wisdom of others who have loved me, saw potential in me and many who have been willing to take a risk on me. Some of these men have been spiritual mentors. Others have taught me how to live life and be a man who is true to his word. All of these men have given of themselves far beyond that which I deserved and for that I am thankful. There are a few of these men who are already with Jesus, but the memories that I hold of them and the legacy that they imparted to me continues to shape me today.

Thank you…

Wayne Reece
Rusty Goe
Charles D. Aldridge
Glenn C. Burris, Sr.
Jack Hatcher
Randy Delp
Johnny Gonzales
Tim Peterson
Glenn Burris, Jr.
Jack Hayford
Dale Downs
David Stogsdill
John Long
Dutch Sheets

I am forever Grateful.

CONTENTS

ACKNOWLEDGMENTS

I want to express my deepest gratitude to Sally Weckel and Anna Kyer for your invaluable assistance in proofreading and editing this book. Your tireless efforts and commitment to excellence are deeply appreciated, as are your hearts for Jesus and His kingdom.

The Lord God Jehovah is a victorious God! He rules and reigns supreme over all of heaven and the earth. He has never been defeated and never will be. Heaven is His throne and the earth is His footstool. All power and authority belong to Him and His scepter is righteousness. As a child of the Father, you were never meant to live a broken down and defeated life. The Bible clearly teaches that we are to rule and reign with Christ in the heavenlies. Jesus defeated satan once and for all and took the keys to death, hell and the grave. He has transferred His authority to the believer and given us the power to live victorious lives. May the word of victory rise up in your spirit and may you begin to walk according to the standard of the word that advances and accelerates you to a life of victorious living.

1. Deuteronomy 20:4

For the Lord your God is he who goes with you to fight for you against your enemies, to give you the victory.

2. Philippians 4:13

I can do all things through him who strengthens me.

3. John 16:33

I have said these things to you, that in me you may have peace. In the world you will have tribulation. But take heart; I have overcome the world."

4. James 1:12-14

Blessed is the man who remains steadfast under trial, for when he has stood the test he will receive the crown of life, which God has promised to those who love him. Let no one say when he is tempted, "I am being tempted by God," for God cannot be tempted with evil, and he himself tempts no one. But each person is tempted when he is lured and enticed by his own desire.

5. Psalm 108:13

With God we shall do valiantly; it is he who will tread down our foes.

6. 1 Corinthians 10:13

No temptation has overtaken you that is not common to man. God is faithful, and he will not let you be tempted beyond your ability, but with the temptation he will also provide the way of escape, that you may be able to endure it.

7. 1 Corinthians 15:57

But thanks be to God, who gives us the victory through our Lord Jesus Christ.

8. Deuteronomy 20:1-4

"When you go out to war against your enemies, and see horses and chariots and an army larger than your own, you shall not be afraid of them, for the Lord your God is with you, who brought you up out of the land of Egypt. And when you draw near to the battle, the priest shall come forward and speak to the people and shall say to them, 'Hear, O Israel, today you are drawing near for battle against your enemies: let not your heart faint.

Do not fear or panic or be in dread of them, for the Lord your God is he who goes with you to fight for you against your enemies, to give you the victory.'

9. 2 Corinthians 12:9-10

But he said to me, "My grace is sufficient for you, for my power is made perfect in weakness." Therefore I will boast all the more gladly of my weaknesses, so that the power of Christ may rest upon me. For the sake of Christ, then, I am content with weaknesses, insults, hardships, persecutions, and calamities. For when I am weak, then I am strong.

10. Ephesians 6:13

Therefore take up the whole armor of God, that you may be able to withstand in the evil day, and having done all, to stand firm.

11. Ephesians 6:10

Finally, be strong in the Lord and in the strength of his might.

12. Proverbs 24:16

For the righteous falls seven times and rises again, but the wicked stumble in times of calamity.

13. Revelation 21:6-7

And he said to me, "It is done! I am the Alpha and the Omega, the beginning and the end. To the thirsty I will give from the spring of the water of life without payment.

The one who conquers will have this heritage, and I will be his God and he will be my son.

14. John 14:26

But the Helper, the Holy Spirit, whom the Father will send in my name, he will teach you all things and bring to your remembrance all that I have said to you.

15. Revelation 12:10

And I heard a loud voice in heaven, saying, "Now the salvation and the power and the kingdom of our God and the authority of his Christ have come, for the accuser of our brothers has been thrown down, who accuses them day and night before our God.

16. James 1:1-27

James, a servant of God and of the Lord Jesus Christ, To the twelve tribes in the Dispersion: Greetings. Count it all joy, my brothers, when you meet trials of various kinds, for you know that the testing of your faith produces steadfastness. And let steadfastness have its full effect, that you may be perfect and complete, lacking in nothing. If any of you lacks wisdom, let him ask God, who gives generously to all without reproach, and it will be given him...

17. Isaiah 41:13

For I, the Lord your God, hold your right hand; it is I who say to you, "Fear not, I am the one who helps you."

18. 2 Peter 3:9

The Lord is not slow to fulfill his promise as some count slowness, but is patient toward you, not wishing that any should perish, but that all should reach repentance.

19. Luke 10:19

Behold, I have given you authority to tread on serpents and scorpions, and over all the power of the enemy, and nothing shall hurt you.

20. Matthew 16:18

And I tell you, you are Peter, and on this rock I will build my church, and the gates of hell shall not prevail against it.

21. 1 John 1:9

If we confess our sins, he is faithful and just to forgive us our sins and to cleanse us from all unrighteousness.

22. 2 Timothy 2:15

Do your best to present yourself to God as one approved, a worker who has no need to be ashamed, rightly handling the word of truth.

23. 1 Peter 3:18

For Christ also suffered once for sins, the righteous for the unrighteous, that he might bring us to God, being put to death in the flesh but made alive in the spirit,

24. James 5:13

Is anyone among you suffering? Let him pray. Is anyone cheerful? Let him sing praise.

25. Hebrews 11:1

Now faith is the assurance of things hoped for, the conviction of things not seen.

26. 1 John 5:4-5

For everyone who has been born of God overcomes the world.

And this is the victory that has overcome the world—our faith. Who is it that overcomes the world except the one who believes that Jesus is the Son of God?

27. 2 Corinthians 10:4

For the weapons of our warfare are not of the flesh but have divine power to destroy strongholds.

28. Romans 8:37

No, in all these things we are more than conquerors through him who loved us.

29. John 3:17

For God did not send his Son into the world to condemn the world, but in order that the world might be saved through him.

30. 1 Chronicles 11:14

But he took his stand in the midst of the plot and defended it and killed the Philistines. And the Lord saved them by a great victory.

31. Genesis 18:14

Is anything too hard for the Lord? At the appointed time I will return to you, about this time next year, and Sarah shall have a son."

32. Psalm 8:2

Out of the mouth of babies and infants, you have established strength because of your foes, to still the enemy and the avenger.

33. 2 Corinthians 5:17

Therefore, if anyone is in Christ, he is a new creation. The old has passed away; behold, the new has come.

34. 2 Corinthians 2:14

But thanks be to God, who in Christ always leads us in triumphal procession, and through us spreads the fragrance of the knowledge of him everywhere.

35. Mark 11:24

Therefore I tell you, whatever you ask in prayer, believe that you have received it, and it will be yours.

36. 1 Corinthians 15:52

In a moment, in the twinkling of an eye, at the last trumpet. For the trumpet will sound, and the dead will be raised imperishable, and we shall be changed.

37. Jeremiah 29:11

For I know the plans I have for you, declares the Lord, plans for welfare and not for evil, to give you a future and a hope.

38. 1 Corinthians 15:51

Behold! I tell you a mystery. We shall not all sleep, but we shall all be changed,

39. John 14:6

Jesus said to him, "I am the way, and the truth, and the life. No one comes to the Father except through me.

40. 1 Samuel 1:1-28

There was a certain man of Ramathaim-zophim of the hill country of Ephraim whose name was Elkanah the son of Jeroham, son of Elihu, son of Tohu, son of Zuph, an Ephrathite. He had two wives. The name of the one was Hannah, and the name of the other, Peninnah. And Peninnah had children, but Hannah had no children. Now this man used to go up year by year from his city to worship and to sacrifice to the Lord of hosts at Shiloh, where the two sons of Eli, Hophni and Phinehas, were priests of the Lord. On the day when Elkanah sacrificed, he would give portions to Peninnah his wife and to all her sons and daughters. But to Hannah he gave a double portion, because he loved her, though the Lord had closed her womb.

41. 1 John 5:4

For everyone who has been born of God overcomes the world. And this is the victory that has overcome the world—our faith.

42. 1 Corinthians 15:55-57

"O death, where is your victory? O death, where is your sting?" The sting of death is sin, and the power of sin is the law. But thanks be to God, who gives us the victory through our Lord Jesus Christ.

43. 1 Thessalonians 4:13-18

But we do not want you to be uninformed, brothers, about those who are asleep, that you may not grieve as others do who have no hope. For since we believe that Jesus died and rose again, even so, through Jesus, God will bring with him those who have fallen asleep. For this we declare to you by a word from the Lord, that we who are alive, who are left until the coming of the Lord, will not precede those who have fallen asleep. For the Lord himself will descend from heaven with a cry of command, with the voice of an archangel, and with the sound of the trumpet of God. And the dead in Christ will rise first. Then we who are alive, who are left, will be caught up together with them in the clouds to meet the Lord in the air, and so we will always be with the Lord.

44. Proverbs 21:31

The horse is made ready for the day of battle, but the victory belongs to the Lord.

45. 1 Samuel 1:1-28:25

There was a certain man of Ramathaim-zophim of the hill country of Ephraim whose name was Elkanah the son of Jeroham, son of Elihu, son of Tohu, son of Zuph, an Ephrathite. He had two wives. The name of the one was Hannah, and the name of the other, Peninnah. And Peninnah had children, but Hannah had no children. Now this man used to go up year by year from his city to worship and to sacrifice to the Lord of hosts at Shiloh, where the two sons of Eli, Hophni and Phinehas, were priests of the Lord. On the day when Elkanah sacrificed, he would give portions to Peninnah his wife and to all her sons and daughters. But to Hannah he gave a double portion, because he loved her, though the Lord had closed her womb. ...

46. Acts 2:27

For you will not abandon my soul to Hades, or let your Holy One see corruption.

47. 1 Corinthians 15:57-58

But thanks be to God, who gives us the victory through our Lord Jesus Christ. Therefore, my beloved brothers, be steadfast, immovable, always abounding in the work of the Lord, knowing that in the Lord your labor is not in vain.

48. 1 Corinthians 15:55

"O death, where is your victory? O death, where is your sting?"

49. Romans 8:31

What then shall we say to these things? If God is for us, who can be against us?

50. John 20:17

Jesus said to her, "Do not cling to me, for I have not yet ascended to the Father; but go to my brothers and say to them, 'I am ascending to my Father and your Father, to my God and your God.'"

51. Luke 16:19-31

"There was a rich man who was clothed in purple and fine linen and who feasted sumptuously every day. And at his gate was laid a poor man named Lazarus, covered with sores, who desired to be fed with what fell from the rich man's table. Moreover, even the dogs came and licked his sores. The poor man died and was carried by the angels to Abraham's side. The rich man also died and was buried, and in Hades, being in torment, he lifted up his eyes and saw Abraham far off and Lazarus at his side. ...

52. Matthew 19:28

Jesus said to them, "Truly, I say to you, in the new world, when the Son of Man will sit on his glorious throne, you who have followed me will also sit on twelve thrones, judging the twelve tribes of Israel.

53. 1 Corinthians 15:22

For as in Adam all die, so also in Christ shall all be made alive.

54. Isaiah 55:9

For as the heavens are higher than the earth, so are my ways higher than your ways and my thoughts than your thoughts.

55. Isaiah 1:1-31

The vision of Isaiah the son of Amoz, which he saw concerning Judah and Jerusalem in the days of Uzziah, Jotham, Ahaz, and Hezekiah, kings of Judah. Hear, O heavens, and give ear, O earth; for the Lord has spoken: "Children have I reared and brought up, but they have rebelled against me. The ox knows its owner, and the donkey its master's crib, but Israel does not know, my people do not understand." Ah, sinful nation, a people laden with iniquity, offspring of evildoers, children who deal corruptly! They have forsaken the Lord, they have despised the Holy One of Israel, they are utterly estranged. Why will you still be struck down? Why will you continue to rebel? The whole head is sick, and the whole heart faint. ...

56. Psalm 60:12

With God we shall do valiantly; it is he who will tread down our foes.

57. Matthew 24:1-51

Jesus left the temple and was going away, when his disciples came to point out to him the buildings of the temple. But he answered them, "You see all these, do you not? Truly, I say to you, there will not be left here one stone upon another that will not be thrown down." As he sat on the Mount of Olives, the disciples came to him privately, saying, "Tell us, when will these things be, and what will be the sign of your coming and of the close of the age?" And Jesus answered them, "See that no one leads you astray. For many will come in my name, saying, 'I am the Christ,' and they will lead many astray. ...

58. Matthew 6:24

"No one can serve two masters, for either he will hate the one and love the other, or he will be devoted to the one and despise the other. You cannot serve God and money.

59. Revelation 12:11

And they have conquered him by the blood of the Lamb and by the word of their testimony, for they loved not their lives even unto death.

60. 2 Timothy 4:7

I have fought the good fight, I have finished the race, I have kept the faith.

61. Romans 8:1-39

There is therefore now no condemnation for those who are in Christ Jesus. For the law of the Spirit of life has set you free in Christ Jesus from the law of sin and death. For God has done what the law, weakened by the flesh, could not do. By sending his own Son in the likeness of sinful flesh and for sin, he condemned sin in the flesh, in order that the righteous requirement of the law might be fulfilled in us, who walk not according to the flesh but according to the Spirit. For those who live according to the flesh set their minds on the things of the flesh, but those who live according to the Spirit set their minds on the things of the Spirit.

62. John 3:16

"For God so loved the world, that he gave his only Son, that whoever believes in him should not perish but have eternal life.

63. Matthew 17:1-9

And after six days Jesus took with him Peter and James, and John his brother, and led them up a high mountain by themselves. And he was transfigured before them, and his face shone like the sun, and his clothes became white as light. And behold, there appeared to them Moses and Elijah, talking with him. And Peter said to Jesus, "Lord, it is good that we are here. If you wish, I will make three tents here, one for you and one for Moses and one for Elijah." He was still speaking when, behold, a bright cloud overshadowed them, and a voice from the cloud said, "This is my beloved Son, with whom I am well pleased; listen to him." ...

64. Revelation 20:1-15

Then I saw an angel coming down from heaven, holding in his hand the key to the bottomless pit and a great chain. And he seized the dragon, that ancient serpent, who is the devil and Satan, and bound him for a thousand years, and threw him into the pit, and shut it and sealed it over him, so that he might not deceive the nations any longer, until the thousand years were ended. After that he must be released for a little while. Then I saw thrones, and seated on them were those to whom the authority to judge was committed. Also I saw the souls of those who had been beheaded for the testimony of Jesus and for the word of God, and those who had not worshiped the beast or its image and had not received its mark on their foreheads or their hands. They came to life and reigned with Christ for a thousand years. The rest of the dead did not come to life until the thousand years were ended. This is the first resurrection.

65. Revelation 11:15

Then the seventh angel blew his trumpet, and there were loud voices in heaven, saying, "The kingdom of the world has become the kingdom of our Lord and of his Christ, and he shall reign forever and ever."

66. 1 John 4:4

Little children, you are from God and have overcome them, for he who is in you is greater than he who is in the world.

67. Ephesians 6:10-18

Finally, be strong in the Lord and in the strength of his might. Put on the whole armor of God, that you may be able to stand against the schemes of the devil. For we do not wrestle against flesh and blood, but against the rulers, against the authorities, against the cosmic powers over this present darkness, against the spiritual forces of evil in the heavenly places. Therefore take up the whole armor of God, that you may be able to withstand in the evil day, and having done all, to stand firm. Stand therefore, having fastened on the belt of truth, and having put on the breastplate of righteousness…"

68. Psalm 66:3

Say to God, "How awesome are your deeds! So great is your power that your enemies come cringing to you.

69. Joshua 10:8

And the Lord said to Joshua, "Do not fear them, for I have given them into your hands. Not a man of them shall stand before you."

70. James 2:19

You believe that God is one; you do well. Even the demons believe—and shudder!

71. Colossians 2:15

He disarmed the rulers and authorities and put them to open shame, by triumphing over them in him.

72. 2 Chronicles 20:17

You will not need to fight in this battle. Stand firm, hold your position, and see the salvation of the Lord on your behalf, O Judah and Jerusalem.' Do not be afraid and do not be dismayed. Tomorrow go out against them, and the Lord will be with you."

73. Genesis 1:1-31

In the beginning, God created the heavens and the earth. The earth was without form and void, and darkness was over the face of the deep. And the Spirit of God was hovering over the face of the waters. And God said, "Let there be light," and there was light. And God saw that the light was good. And God separated the light from the darkness. God called the light Day, and the darkness he called Night. And there was evening and there was morning, the first day. ...

74. Revelation 14:10

He also will drink the wine of God's wrath, poured full strength into the cup of his anger, and he will be tormented with fire and sulfur in the presence of the holy angels and in the presence of the Lamb.

75. Revelation 1:1-20

The revelation of Jesus Christ, which God gave him to show to his servants the things that must soon take place. He made it known by sending his angel to his servant John, who bore witness to the word of God and to the testimony of Jesus Christ, even to all that he saw. Blessed is the one who reads aloud the words of this prophecy, and blessed are those who hear, and who keep what is written in it, for the time is near. John to the seven churches that are in Asia: Grace to you and peace from him who is and who was and who is to come, and from the seven spirits who are before his throne, and from Jesus Christ the faithful witness, the firstborn of the dead, and the ruler of kings on earth. To him who loves us and has freed us from our sins by his blood ...

76. Romans 8:1

There is therefore now no condemnation for those who are in Christ Jesus.

77. Romans 1:1

Paul, a servant of Christ Jesus, called to be an apostle, set apart for the gospel of God,

78. 2 Chronicles 32:7

"Be strong and courageous. Do not be afraid or dismayed before the king of Assyria and all the horde that is with him, for there are more with us than with him.

79. Revelation 17:8

The beast that you saw was, and is not, and is about to rise from the bottomless pit and go to destruction. And the dwellers on earth whose names have not been written in the book of life from the foundation of the world will marvel to see the beast, because it was and is not and is to come.

80. 1 John 4:1

Beloved, do not believe every spirit, but test the spirits to see whether they are from God, for many false prophets have gone out into the world.

81. Romans 8:31-32

What then shall we say to these things? If God is for us, who can be against us? He who did not spare his own Son but gave him up for us all, how will he not also with him graciously give us all things?

82. John 8:44

You are of your father the devil, and your will is to do your father's desires. He was a murderer from the beginning, and has nothing to do with the truth, because there is no truth in him. When he lies, he speaks out of his own character, for he is a liar and the father of lies.

83. Matthew 7:21-23

"Not everyone who says to me, 'Lord, Lord,' will enter the kingdom of heaven, but the one who does the will of my Father who is in heaven. On that day many will say to me, 'Lord, Lord, did we not prophesy in your name, and cast out demons in your name, and do many mighty works in your name?' And then will I declare to them, 'I never knew you; depart from me, you workers of lawlessness.'

84. Psalm 3:8

Salvation belongs to the Lord; your blessing be on your people! Selah

85. Revelation 21:4

He will wipe away every tear from their eyes, and death shall be no more, neither shall there be mourning, nor crying, nor pain anymore, for the former things have passed away."

86. Revelation 3:11

I am coming soon. Hold fast what you have, so that no one may seize your crown.

87. 1 Peter 2:9

But you are a chosen race, a royal priesthood, a holy nation, a people for his own possession, that you may proclaim the excellencies of him who called you out of darkness into his marvelous light.

88. 1 Thessalonians 4:17

Then we who are alive, who are left, will be caught up together with them in the clouds to meet the Lord in the air, and so we will always be with the Lord.

89. Romans 8:38-39

For I am sure that neither death nor life, nor angels nor rulers, nor things present nor things to come, nor powers, nor height nor depth, nor anything else in all creation, will be able to separate us from the love of God in Christ Jesus our Lord.

90. Romans 6:14

For sin will have no dominion over you, since you are not under law but under grace.

91. 2 Kings 5:1

Naaman, commander of the army of the king of Syria, was a great man with his master and in high favor, because by him the Lord had given victory to Syria. He was a mighty man of valor, but he was a leper.

92. 1 Samuel 2:8

He raises up the poor from the dust; he lifts the needy from the ash heap to make them sit with princes and inherit a seat of honor. For the pillars of the earth are the Lord's, and on them he has set the world.

93. 1 John 5:1-21

Everyone who believes that Jesus is the Christ has been born of God, and everyone who loves the Father loves whoever has been born of him. By this we know that we love the children of God, when we love God and obey his commandments. For this is the love of God, that we keep his commandments. And his commandments are not burdensome. For everyone who has been born of God overcomes the world. And this is the victory that has overcome the world—our faith. Who is it that overcomes the world except the one who believes that Jesus is the Son of God?

94. 1 John 3:8

Whoever makes a practice of sinning is of the devil, for the devil has been sinning from the beginning. The reason the Son of God appeared was to destroy the works of the devil.

95. 1 Peter 5:8

Be sober-minded; be watchful. Your adversary the devil prowls around like a roaring lion, seeking someone to devour.

96. James 1:12

Blessed is the man who remains steadfast under trial, for when he has stood the test he will receive the crown of life, which God has promised to those who love him.

97. Hebrews 13:6

So we can confidently say, "The Lord is my helper; I will not fear; what can man do to me?"

98. Hebrews 4:12

For the word of God is living and active, sharper than any two-edged sword, piercing to the division of soul and of spirit, of joints and of marrow, and discerning the thoughts and intentions of the heart.

99. John 19:30

When Jesus had received the sour wine, he said, "It is finished," and he bowed his head and gave up his spirit.

100. Isaiah 46:4

Even to your old age I am he, and to gray hairs I will carry you. I have made, and I will bear; I will carry and will save.

Day One

THE WAR OF NINE KINGS

"And it came to pass in the days of Amraphel king of Shinar, Arioch king of Ellasar, Chedorlaomer king of Elam, and Tidal king of nations, that they made war with Bera king of Sodom, Birsha king of Gomorrah, Shinab king of Admah, Shemeber king of Zeboiim, and the king of Bela (that is, Zoar). All these joined together in the Valley of Siddim (that is, the Salt Sea). Twelve years they served Chedorlaomer, and in the thirteenth year they rebelled."

Genesis 14:1-17

This interesting story involving nine kings is the very first battle mentioned in the Bible. It ultimately involved Abraham, but in actuality it wasn't his battle. As is often the case with kings, this battle was about control, territory, strength and conquest. King Chedorlaomer of Elam was in alliance with three other kings, comprising the rule over Mesopotamia and held control over the region of the Jordan plain. Five other kings, who were the subject of this control, decided to create an alliance of their own and stand up to him. Our focus and interest in this battle isn't necessarily these kings, their reasons for battle or really even the outcome. We become interested when the conquering kings make a mistake and crossed the line when they kidnap the nephew (and his family) of Abraham.

King Chedorlaomer attacked Sodom and Gomorrah where Abraham's nephew, just happened to live. There are several "teaching points" that can be gleaned from this historical battle, but the very first has to be the battleground itself. In resistance against the attacker, the five kings in alliance chose to fight in the

"Valley of Siddim," which was a part of the Dead Sea that had begun to dry out. The Siddim valley was full of tar and asphalt slime pits, and proved to be disastrous for the armies of Sodom and Gomorrah. The soldiers, their horses and chariots got stuck in these pits, both accidentally as well as intentionally as the Mesopotamian armies drove them further into the "pits of despair."

With their forces now severely weakened, the remaining armies fled to Sodom and Gomorrah where they were easily overtaken, seized and captured. The mistake the Mesopotamians made was that in seizing the spoils of war and the citizens of the city, (intending to enslave them), they kidnapped an unknown citizen named Lot, who happened to be the nephew of Abraham. Once Abraham was made aware of the situation, he launched a counter attack with 318 of his "servants." Going against an army of thousands, he successfully rescued Lot and his family, all those that had been captured, as well as the spoils of war that had been taken.

Lessons of Victory

Where you fight matters. The kings of Jordan met the opposition in the Valley of Siddim. Their location strategy served to draw the enemy away from the city population, but the tar pits and asphalt slime endangered the troops and ultimately became their downfall. When you engage the enemy, it is important that you stand on firm ground and not become isolated from that which strengthens you and gives you an advantage. Being and staying in the right place, at the right time, surrounded by the right people is a strategic warfare tactic that will serve to your advantage and victory.

He was Faithful to Family. Prior to this attack, Abraham and Lot had a family disagreement in which Lot took advantage of Abraham. Upon their separation, Lot chose the choice livestock, and the prime real estate. Abraham had every right to leave Lot to his own devices and not to come to his rescue. We are all familiar with the term, "you made your bed, now sleep in it." However, that wasn't Abraham's sentiment. Regardless of their differences, Abraham rescued and delivered one of his family members. He stood up for family and even put his own life in danger to come to the assistance of a family member who needed him. Taking care of family, whether blood or spiritual is a priority of the kingdom. We must stand together, fight together, love together and protect one another at all costs. We are family!

You are not just a Servant, you are a Soldier. There are many metaphors that describe the Christian life. The 318 soldiers who defeated the Mesopotamian armies were also referred to as the servants of Abraham. In reality, they may have functioned in both roles, but the important thing is that when they were called upon, they were ready to fight. And fight they did! They functioned in their role as servants, but they were also armed and battle ready. In the Christian life, you never know when you are going to be called upon to fight, or when you might be attacked. Ephesians tells us to put on the armor of God daily, and to be ready and on alert at all times.

Abraham was bold, confident and courageous. The Bible account isn't clear whether or not Abraham knew the odds that were against him. However, as a man who had 318 highly trained warriors in his personal employ, you can only assume that he understood the tactics of warfare and what he was up against. Despite the odds, he was willing to risk it all to save his family members. The more we learn about Abraham, we find that he was a man of great trust and faith. From that, came a great courage that was willing to attack the enemy. Throughout the scriptures, we are told to "fear not" (Isaiah 41:10).

You can't walk in faith and fear at the same time and without a willingness to stand up and fight for what belongs to you, you will become an easy prey for the enemy.

Abraham had a strategy. Three specific strategic actions marked the success of Abraham's counter-attack. He only used his best-trained warriors, he intentionally pursued the Mesopotamians at night, and he flanked them on multiple sides. His strategy worked and God brought confusion into the enemy's camp. As a result, he recovered all of those who had been captured as well as the valuables and spoils that had been taken from the city. God is not the author of confusion and He always has a divine strategy. Oftentimes, His strategy doesn't make sense to the natural mind, but the weapons of our warfare are not carnal, but mighty through God to the pulling down of strongholds. Seeking God for His strategy not only gives you the victory, but can save your life and the lives of those that are engaged in the warfare with you.

TODAY'S CONFESSION OF VICTORY

I confess today that I am what God says I am. I have what He says I have and I can do what He says I can do. I am not moved by what I see, think, hear or feel. My life is not up for grabs and I have been born for such a time as this. My life is important and who I am counts. I will not allow the enemy to ravage my life, my family, my destiny and my purpose in life. I surround myself with the right people, at the right time, doing the right thing and together we are a mighty force against the schemes and strategies of the enemy. God uses my life to protect those that are important to me. I am a force to be reckoned with and because of my life and testimony, salvation comes to my household. I am training to reign and I live out of the strength of my spirit man. I am not tossed to and fro and am not blinded by the lies of darkness. I am bold, confident and courageous and I walk in the strategy of the word and I am confident in who I am in Christ.

Day Two

THE BATTLE OF THE ARK

"Then the LORD said to Noah, 'Come into the ark, you and all your household, because I have seen that you are righteous before Me in this generation. You shall take with you seven each of every clean animal, a male and his female; two each of animals that are unclean, a male and his female; also seven each of birds of the air, male and female, to keep the species alive on the face of all the earth. For after seven more days I will cause it to rain on the earth forty days and forty nights, and I will destroy from the face of the earth all living things that I have made.' And Noah did according to all that the LORD commanded him. Noah was six hundred years old when the floodwaters were on the earth."

Genesis 7:1-9

The entirety of the globe - all of its inhabitants, all of mankind, all of God's very creation is at stake. Satan has sunk his teeth into every element of society and evil is rampant throughout the earth. Violence, debauchery and corruption have filled the earth and God has had His fill. "The end of all flesh has come before Me, for the earth is filled with violence through them; and behold, I will destroy them with the earth." (Genesis 6:13). The very future of mankind lies in the balance and God needs a man. In most of earth's battles, man needs God's intervention, but in one of the most important battles ever known on the planet, God needs a man to intervene on His behalf. God is looking for a man who can righteously intervene and serve His plans and purposes in the birthing of a new world. Noah was the man that God was looking for. Three distinct characteristics marked the life of Noah that made him the candidate that God was looking for. He was a just man, perfect in his generation and walked with God.

In obeying God, Noah faced seemingly, insurmountable odds. He was the ridicule of society, a supposed derelict from those who lived in rebellion to the ways of God, and quite a madman to those who refused to submit to the authority of God on the earth. Armed with a divine blueprint and a vision that transcended the earthly, Noah set himself to build the world's first ocean liner. His salvation, that of his family and the rescue of mankind literally depended on his success in following a God that nobody could see, nobody wanted to listen to and certainly nobody wanted to obey.

Noah had clearly heard the word of the Lord, and despite the fact that all of society rebelled against everything that was in his heart, he pressed forward in obedience to build an ark. Unbeknownst to Noah's family, the residents of the Ark would be the seed of a new nation, the hope of heaven and the beginning of a new world order. Having completed the tremendous undertaking of building the Ark, the rains of heaven opened upon the earth in unprecedented manner. The waters of the deep burst open and the earth was flooded exactly as the Lord told Noah and in the manner that Noah predicted and warned the people. Everything on the earth, except for the residents of the Ark perished. The battle is over, the war has been won and the casualties are historical. Evil has been defeated and divine expectancy is floating around in an oversized boat filled with animals of every kind and a man and his family who heard the Lord and dared to obey.

Lessons of Victory

Noah had a relationship with God. Genesis 6:8, "Noah found grace in the eyes of the Lord." The grace that Noah walked in before God was favor and acceptance. It wasn't that Noah was "more special" than anybody else, for this was a grace that was available to all of mankind, and in fact, still is. What set Noah apart from the rest of mankind on the earth was that he chose to walk before God, he was just and perfect in his passions to serve God. God was able to use Noah because of his heart. To the degree that you have relationship with God is the degree that you will walk in authority before Him. God greatly desires to fellowship with His children. He desires to be in close fellowship with you! Noah had captured the very essence of what God lost when Adam and Eve sinned in the garden. It is what set Noah apart, made him a candidate for divine intervention and set him up for success and safety. It is no different today with you and I. The strength of battle belongs to those who walk relationally before the Lord.

He obeyed God even when it didn't make sense. Rain? The world at that point had never seen rain that fell from the sky. They had never seen a boat of this magnitude. They had no concept of a God who could speak to them and give them divine directions and they certainly could not imagine the world flooding and destroying every living creature on the earth. Nothing that Noah was doing made logical sense and he became the mockery of society. Despite all that was against him, he obeyed what was in his heart.

God does not always make sense. His word is not always logical or falls within our comfort zone. He uses the foolish things of the world to confound the wise (1 Corinthians 1:27). The key to victory is to set your heart to obey God no matter how contrary it might seem to your natural senses or your carnal mind. Success is found in submission.

God can use an ordinary, old man to save the world. Prior to this story, the name of Noah is never mentioned. He was over 500 years old, and never once did he do anything in his life that was necessarily worthy of biblical press. He was just a faithful man, living his life and raising his family, but when it really counted, he stepped up to the plate. From the time that Noah heard the word of the Lord to the time that the flood came was 120 years. That's a long time to live under the ridicule and torment of a godless society of whom Noah was the mockery. He was patient and stayed the course.

God isn't looking for the superstar to do His will and build His kingdom. He uses ordinary people who will be faithful to Him, submit to His word and trust Him with the future, no matter how contrary it might seem to the onlookers and naysayers. Your greatest ability is your availability and it's in your simple obedience that God is magnified and is able to work in you and through you.

TODAY'S CONFESSION OF VICTORY

Here am I, Lord, use me! Today I set myself to be a man or woman that walks before God in intimate relationship. The most important thing that I can do with my life is to seek and know the heart of the Father. Regardless of the direction of society, I will be found faithful in my generation and I will be the person that goes against the norm if it means that following God demands it. I am an Ark builder. My life is a place of safety for those who are in the storms of life. My God is my stronghold, my safety and security. He is my hope and my salvation. Even though the storms of life may come, I will be safe as I hide myself in God and obey His word. I will not give up!

No matter how difficult the task may be, how long it takes to complete it and no matter how misunderstood I am. I set my hand to the plow and I will not look back. I choose to be faithful to the task and to expect the outcome of God's plans and purposes.

Day Three

THE ULTIMATE SACRIFICE

"Now it came to pass after these things that God tested Abraham, and said to him, "Abraham!" And he said, "Here I am." Then He said, "Take now your son, your only son Isaac, whom you love, and go to the land of Moriah, and offer him there as a burnt offering on one of the mountains of which I shall tell you."

So Abraham rose early in the morning and saddled his donkey, and took two of his young men with him, and Isaac his son; and he split the wood for the burnt offering, and arose and went to the place of which God had told him. Then on the third day Abraham lifted his eyes and saw the place afar off. And Abraham said to his young men, "Stay here with the donkey; the lad and I will go yonder and worship, and we will come back to you."

Genesis 22:1-5

Abraham was a man that walked in obedient faith to God. All that he possessed belonged to God and as a result, He is called the Father of faith. At the age of 100, God blessed him with his promised son, Isaac. Abraham deeply loved Isaac and favored him above all others. He was the son of promise, born to him by Sarah, his beloved wife.

Little does Abraham know that he is going to be tested beyond his wildest imagination! God is going to ask of him the very life of his son.

God speaks to Abraham to travel to Moriah and offer his son as a burnt offering on a very specific mountain. Today, that mountain is called Temple Mount, in the very center of Jerusalem, and is the same mountain upon which Solomon's temple was built. Abraham must be in a state of shock! Why would God demand such a high price of obedience? How can he live without his son of promise? While the Bible isn't clear about Abraham's state of mind, it is clear about the condition of his heart. He responded with absolute faith and resolve. It is evident from Abraham's response that he had a conviction that God would raise his son from the dead if necessary.

With a heart of purity and obedience, Abraham and Isaac made their way to the top of Moriah. He prepared the altar, readied the fire and bound his son as a sacrificial offering unto the Lord. One can only imagine the fear in Isaac, and the confusion in Abraham. Through sweat, tears and exhaustion, Abraham raised the knife to plunge into the heart of his son, when God called out to him from heaven and stopped him from the worst moment of his life.

The angel said, "Do not lay your hand on the lad, or do anything to him; for now I know that you fear God, since you have not withheld your son, your only son, from Me."

Lessons of Victory

Abraham was being tested, not tempted. God is not capable of tempting His children, but He will test them. The testing of God is a valuable thing. Throughout the Bible, the word translated "test" means "to prove by trial." God was proving the faith of Abraham because the magnitude of what he was being called to demanded that he be tested beyond anything that he had experienced to date. Quite often, I drive over bridges that have a sign indicating the load capacity. The small sign is a message to drivers that if you have a load that exceeds the capacity of the bridge, it could be dangerous. God wasn't testing Abraham for

His own sake, because He already knew his heart. He was proving to Abraham that he had a load capacity that would qualify him as the "father of faith" and a "father to the nations." The testing of the Lord is always for the purposes of promotion and acceleration. In the midst of testing, we often find that God is purifying our faith, perfecting our character or protecting us from sin. To be obedient, even in the most difficult test is to posture yourself for the promotion of God in your life.

Focus on the Promise. God never had to explain His reasoning to Abraham. He trusted God and walked in a conviction that his son of promise would fulfill the covenant that God had entered into with him. His confidence was in the covenant, and he knew that God was a covenant keeping God. In keeping covenant, God always redeems His promises. If He had a reason and a purpose for taking the life of Isaac, Abraham was confident that God would restore him and raise him up again. Faith never demands that God explain Himself, but simply trusts in the promise. Abraham believed God even when he didn't know where, when, how or why.

This sacrificial offering was a type and shadow. In this story, Abraham is representative of the Father God and Isaac is representative of Jesus. Both of them worked together to accomplish a pattern that would actually be fulfilled in the sacrificial offering of Jesus Christ. The Father asked nothing of Abraham that He wasn't willing to do Himself. In fact, He was not only willing, He actually did sacrifice His only Son. In the case of Isaac, God mercifully provided a substitute offering, but the blood of Jesus was required in order to redeem mankind. There would be no substitute. Like Jesus, Isaac bore the burden of sin to the place of the sacrifice. The wood was laid upon Isaac, even as the cross was laid upon Jesus. Finally, although he did not actually die, Isaac was raised up from the place destined for his death. Jesus actually did die, and was supernaturally raised up from the dead.

Abraham's faith was rewarded. A good farmer knows exactly how he ends up with a good harvest. Every season begins with an anticipation of the harvest. He plows the ground with the expectation of seed being planted; he plants the seed with the expectation of harvest. When we walk in faith, there should always be the expectation of the "reward of faith" (1 Peter 1:5-9). Because Abraham was obedient to the Father, he was blessed beyond measure! Genesis 22:15-18, "Then the Angel of the LORD called to Abraham a second time out of heaven, and said: "By Myself I have sworn, says the LORD, because you have done this thing, and have not withheld your son, your only son— blessing I will bless you, and multiplying I will multiply your descendants as the stars of the heaven and as the sand which is on the seashore; and your descendants shall possess the gate of their enemies. In your seed all the nations of the earth shall be blessed, because you have obeyed My voice."

TODAY'S CONFESSION OF VICTORY

All that I am, all that I ever have been and ever will be belongs to You. I surrender my heart, my life, my passions, my will and my destiny into Your heart and hands. I trust You completely and fully. I thank You that like Isaac, I am a son of promise and I walk in the divine favor and purposes of my Father. My life is unique, my calling is distinctive and You have raised me up for such a time as this. I have the discernment to know when I am being tested of the Lord or tempted of the enemy. I will not turn my heart away from God's proving processes in my life, but I will fully submit to every plan and purpose that He has for me. I know that my testing is for the purposes of my promotion and acceleration in life. I thank You, Lord that Your promises over me are yes, and amen! You are the giver of all good things, and I walk in the power of Your promise and the redemptive rights that belong to me as Your child. I have a divine expectancy of the seeds of faith that I plant and I anticipate the abundance of harvest as a result of my seed, in Jesus' Name!

Day Four

ALL FOR A BOWL OF BEANS

*"Now Jacob cooked a stew; and Esau came in from the field, and
he was weary. And Esau said to Jacob, "Please feed me with that same
red stew, for I am weary." Therefore his name was called Edom. But
Jacob said, "Sell me your birthright as of this day." And Esau said,
"Look, I am about to die; so what is this birthright to me?" Then Jacob
said, "Swear to me as of this day." So he swore to him, and sold his
birthright to Jacob. And Jacob gave Esau bread and stew of lentils; then
he ate and drank, arose, and went his way. Thus Esau
despised his birthright."*

Genesis 25:29-34

Esau has had a long day in the fields hunting. Up since the early
morning hours, it hasn't been a successful or rewarding day for
the hunter. This is not a man who is a stranger to living off the
land, but this day has not paid off. As he makes his way back
home, he is tired, thirsty, hungry and weary. The long hike home,
empty-handed, makes the day even worse. As he nears familiar
territory, a welcome aroma fills the air and beckons him
homeward. Could it be? His twin brother is cooking one of his
favorite meals! Jacob has mastered the recipe from his mother and
his lentil stew is second to none. Anticipation rises in Esau's heart,
but little does he know that he's being set up.

Jacob isn't just busy making yet another pot of stew. He is making
a stew that holds a deceptive key to his future. He has a plan in
operation that will take advantage of his brother's impulsive and
narcissistic manner of life.

While Esau is concerned about filling up an empty belly, Jacob has crafted a plan that will posture him to steal his brother's birthright. Esau doesn't think much of the matter, and he flippantly gives up a double portion of his father's goods, the rank as patriarch of the family, and priest of the house. Ultimately, this one decision over a bowl of beans cost him unimaginable wealth, power, military might, political influence, and literally world leadership. Little could he have realized that North America, Australia, New Zealand, and South Africa, vast sections of Europe, and parts of the Middle East, would all be a part of the promise of Abraham that he was giving up in a moment of carnal appetite.

Esau never even considered the spiritual influence and the blessing that accompanied the birthright. He was too caught up in the present reality of his hunger to think about the future. The only thing that he could focus on was his immediate need to satisfy his appetite.

His impulsive reaction cost him and his descendants dearly. One of the saddest verses in the Bible references Esau, "Thus Esau despised his birthright." (Genesis 25:34).

Lessons of Victory

Our lessons in victory today are more about what not to do, as we pursue victory in our battles. We can learn more from Esau than we can from Jacob in this situation.

You're not THAT hungry. This is one of the most unfortunate stories in the Bible. Here we have a man with every right to become one of the most powerful, influential and richest men in history, yet he gave all of that up for nothing more than a bowl of beans. This has to be the costliest lunch in the history of the world! Stop and think about what is really happening here. Esau is no longer in the field, but close to home. He's not really that far away from being able to secure another meal, if only he had been patient. The lesson found here is to control your appetites, and we're not just talking about food. If you don't learn how to control your passions and appetites, they will control you. The person that cannot control their appetites is like a city that has no borders, or no protection (Proverbs 25:28). The scripture actually refers to that person as one who "has no rule over his own spirit."

Always know what is at stake. It's not clear in this story if Esau fully understood what his birthright was, but one thing is for certain – Jacob clearly knew. The birthright was the natural privilege of the firstborn son. Receiving the birthright, the firstborn would become the head of the household, and would have charge of the family, including the family property. He would exercise considerable authority over the other members of the family. The blessing that he received would also place him in a special covenant relationship with the Lord. During the Patriarchal period when Jacob and Esau lived, God dealt directly with the heads of the families. The Hebrews counted the blessing given by the father to be very important and considered it an oral contract, which was just as binding as a written contract. As stated earlier, Esau gave up unspeakable wealth, influence, political power, military might as for a well-cooked lunch.

Your decisions now, can affect others later. The descendants of Esau were called the Edomites. They were a people that desperately struggled in life. The properties that Esau did inherit were turned into wastelands, and his inheritance consumed by the desert jackals (Malachi 1:3). Esau eventually despised even the blessing that his father bestowed upon him and effectively became a godless man, with his descendants following suit. Hebrews judges him rather harshly: "See that no one is sexually immoral, or is godless like Esau, who for a single meal sold his inheritance rights as the oldest son. Afterward, as you know, when he wanted to inherit this blessing, he was rejected. Even though he sought the blessing with tears, he could not change what he had done." (Hebrews 12:16-17).

The Edomites became a pagan society and worshipped fertility gods. They were conquered many times over by many different nations and kings and always held to a deep hatred for Israel. One of the best-known descendants of Esau was a man who was appointed King of Judea, known in history as King Herod the Great, the tyrant who ordered a massacre in Bethlehem in an attempt to kill the Christ child (Matthew 2:16-18). The more you discover about Esau and his descendants, the more you realize the great mistake he made in giving up his precious birthright, for nothing more than a bowl of beans!

TODAY'S CONFESSION OF VICTORY

Lord, may my heart be filled with an unquenchable appetite for you! Only you can satisfy the deepest longings of my soul. Only you can cause me to eat the bread of life that eternally sustains and drink the water that will cause me never to thirst again. I declare today that I will not be under the rule or heavy hand of my carnal desires and longings. I am not ruled by my carnal appetites and I will not be consumed by that which is temporal. I put the protective wall of the word around my life and I am not up for grabs.

My heart, my soul and my spirit are surrounded by the word and from the word, I find life, health, healing, wholeness, victory, protection and pleasure. You God, are more than enough!

Day Five

THE WRESTLING MATCH

"And he arose that night and took his two wives, his two female servants, and his eleven sons, and crossed over the ford of Jabbok. He took them, sent them over the brook, and sent over what he had. Then Jacob was left alone; and a Man wrestled with him until the breaking of day. Now when He saw that He did not prevail against him, He touched the socket of his hip; and the socket of Jacob's hip was out of joint as He wrestled with him. And He said, "Let Me go, for the day breaks." But he said, "I will not let You go unless You bless me!" So He said to him, "What is your name?" He said, "Jacob." And He said, "Your name shall no longer be called Jacob, but Israel; for you have struggled with God and with men, and have prevailed."

GENESIS 32:22-28

This is one of the most unusual stories in the Bible! Jacob actually wrestled with God and lived to tell the story. Since this is more of a devotional book rather than a study of theology, it will simply suffice to say that the only way that Jacob could have wrestled with God and lived, is that God uniquely disguised Himself to the degree that Jacob was able to look upon Him. This was not the night that Jacob had imagined. On his way to meet his brother, Esau, he is already filled with dread, not knowing the disposition of his brother or what is before him. He has deceived his brother and taken both his birthright and blessing. He is not sure if his brother is angry and planning to strike back at him and his family, or not.

With this uncertainty heavy on his heart, he is spending a restless night beside the river Jabbok. Jabbok means "outpouring" and that's where Jacob finds himself. He is pouring out his heart to God both in terms of his immediate concern with his brother as well as the future and destiny of his family. In the middle of the night, a stranger shows up in Jacob's camp and actually begins wrestling with him. This is no insignificant wrestling match, but one that would endure throughout the night and into the morning hours. Jacob is exhausted, but he gives it his all and the stranger does not prevail against him. In a seemingly unfair move, the stranger touches the socket of Jacob's hip and literally causes his hip joint to be out of place. Even then, Jacob doesn't give up and the stranger calls for a break at sunrise. Apparently, by now Jacob realizes that his wrestling partner is no ordinary man and he makes a conditional promise; "I will let you go, but not until you bless me." (Verse 26). And bless him, he did!

The Lord not only blessed Jacob, but also changed his name. Jacob means "one who deceives," while Israel in its most basic meaning is "one who is triumphant with God" or "who prevails with God." Commentators will differ on the original literal meaning of the name, but some of the common, agreed upon meanings are "to rule, to be strong; have authority over." Other possible meanings include "the prince of God" as well as "God rules." In one wrestling match, God changed his character, his purpose and his destiny.

Lessons of Victory

Take a time out. Jacob was in a place of uncertainty with his back against the wall. With a history of deceptive practices towards his brother, he was not sure of what was going to transpire between the two of them when they met. He was already stinging due to a negative relational fallout with his father-in-law and the last thing he wants or needs is more conflict from his brother. In the midst of all his family turmoil, he finds himself at the river Jabbok. It is time to pour out to the Lord all of his concerns, fears and uncertainties. Most of us have been in these positions before and often find ourselves at the mercy of our own emotions or the emotions of others. A time out can help you sort through the emotions, get a fresh or different perspective and put things back in order.

Jacob was being broken. We live in a society where value is placed on perfection, photo-shopping is the norm and artificial beauty taunts our children. The concept of brokenness is neither promoted nor understood by most, yet it is a principle of the kingdom that Jesus lived and taught. Then Jesus said to His disciples, "If anyone desires to come after Me, let him deny himself, and take up his cross, and follow Me. For whoever desires to save his life will lose it, but whoever loses his life for My sake will find it." (Matthew 16:24-25). It is through brokenness that the true riches of who you are find their way to the surface of your life. Like Jacob, most of us live our lives with "us" at the center. When we allow ourselves to become broken, we deal a death-blow to our pride and self-centeredness. Jacob needed a character change if he was going to become the man and the leader that God had destined him to become. As long as his world revolved around himself, he would be disqualified from finishing the race well. Brokenness is being fully surrendered to God, and dying to self. A person who is crucified with Christ has no right to self-pity, bitterness, or retaliation. Since dead men have no rights, there is no place for fighting, fuming, fretting, complaining or the demanding of personal rights.

Brokenness is shattering my will so that all my responses are filled with the Holy Spirit. It wasn't until Moses smote the rock that water came forth. The life and love of God can only come forth from broken people. Brokenness is our response of humility and obedience to the conviction of God's Spirit or the revelation of His Word.

But brokenness must also include obedience. Acknowledging sin is not enough! We must obey! Obedience is instantly doing all God tells me to do with the right heart attitude.

Finding God in the struggle. It's not clear at what point Jacob knew He was wrestling with God. Eventually, it dawned on him that this was a night of divine intervention. At the break of dawn, when asked to end the match, he responded with a brilliant request to be blessed. Over and over, the Bible reveals that God is a redeeming God. In 1 Kings 20, the Israelites find themselves in battle against the Syrians, whom they had already soundly defeated in the mountainous regions. As the Syrians assessed the battle (and their defeat), they erroneously concluded that it was due to the fact that the God of Israel was a god of the mountains, but not the valleys. They regrouped, and with a new strategy attacked Israel from the valley and once again were defeated. The learning point of this story is that God is Lord over the mountains and valleys. When you go through the dark times in life, He is a very present help. When you face unbelievable odds, He will never leave you nor forsake you.

There are lessons to be learned in every struggle of life and even when you are not victorious in your battles, you can emerge with a new sense of purpose, life and direction. Jesus is Lord over your life in the dark, in the day and even when the storms rage.

TODAY'S CONFESSION OF VICTORY

I confess that my life is littered with decisions and actions that are less than pleasing to the Lord. I have been self-centered and focused on what is best for me. Through it all, God has had a plan for my life and has invested the deep riches of His word on the inside of me. Lord, I submit to the breaking process of Your gentle hand. You tell me in Your word to take Your yoke upon myself and learn of You. I choose today to take up my cross and follow You. Help me not to rush into the events and affairs of life without stopping to meet with You and pour out my heart to You. May Your hand of grace and mercy rest upon me all the days of my life, whether in the good times, the bad times and even when I'm engaged in the battles of life.

Day Six

FROM PIT TO PALACE

*"So it came to pass, when Joseph had come to his brothers, that they
stripped Joseph of his tunic, the tunic of many colors that was on him.
Then they took him and cast him into a pit. And the
pit was empty; there was no water in it. And they sat down to eat a
meal. Then they lifted their eyes and looked, and there was a company of
Ishmaelites, coming from Gilead with their camels, bearing spices, balm,
and myrrh, on their way to carry them down to Egypt. So Judah said to
his brothers, "What profit is there if we kill our brother and conceal his
blood? Come and let us sell him to the Ishmaelites, and let not our hand
be upon him, for he is our brother and our flesh." And his brothers
listened. Then Midianite traders passed by; so the brothers pulled Joseph
up and lifted him out of the pit, and sold him to the Ishmaelites for
twenty shekels of silver. And they took Joseph to Egypt."*

Genesis 37, 39-42

I would like to take the opportunity to make one thing very clear
regarding Joseph. You most likely won't read this in the majority
of theological commentaries, but Joseph was probably a brat, and
lived a spoiled and favored life. Israel had a special place in his
heart for Joseph as he was the "son of his old age." (Genesis 37:3).
Joseph probably enjoyed being a favored child and most likely
flaunted it in the face of his brothers who grew to hate him. On
top of everything else, Joseph continued to have dreams of
greatness and dominion over his brothers and parents, and was
not shy to share with them with the family. That caused his
brothers to hate him even more.

Despite the immaturity that came with his youthfulness, Joseph was set apart by the Lord for greatness. He was marked with destiny and would one day be the "salvation" of his family and country. God's hand was upon him. Not just for his own sake but also for all who would benefit from the place of favor that was given to him. Joseph would pay a high price for the lofty promotions that he would receive. He would live for years separated from his family and his country, but we find a deep heart of character, passion and purpose that compelled Joseph to be a man that God could use to save a nation.

This story clearly reveals a man who has the mighty hand of God resting upon him. "And the Lord was with Joseph, and he was a prosperous man." (Genesis 39:2). "And his master saw that the Lord was with him, and that the Lord made all that he did to prosper in his hand." (Genesis 39:3). The journey that Joseph finds himself on will affect hundreds of thousands of people. His obedience to the Lord will literally mean life or death for a nation. At every turn and every test, he is being readied for the next great adventure. He never does anything in order to be promoted, he is only faithful to his God and is obedient at every step along the way.

Lessons of Victory

Joseph released his anointing into the lives of others. "So it was, from the time that he had made him overseer of his house and all that he had, that the LORD blessed the Egyptian's house for Joseph's sake; and the blessing of the LORD was on all that he had in the house and in the field." (Genesis 39:5). The "divine overflow" of God was evident upon Joseph's life. Everything that he did had the blessing of God upon it. It showed up on his job and affected everyone and everything that he came into contact with. God wants to bless you so that you can bless others. The company you work for, the church you attend, the neighborhood you live in, the school you attend, the club you belong to; all should be blessed because of your involvement. Do not hold back the blessing from others. Seek ways to cause others to prosper. Look for ways that you can bless other people. There is plenty of God's blessing to go around!

He turned his tests into his testimony. Joseph had plenty of reasons to become bitter, angry and rejected. He could have spent his time groveling in his misfortune and living as an outcast and a stranger in a foreign land, instead, he made the most of his life. No matter what circumstance he found himself in, he was the very best that he could be. He kept a good attitude, remained faithful to the Lord, maintained a pure heart and stayed true to himself. Even as a slave, he refused to have a slave-mentality. He never became a shackled man in his emotions or his outlook in life. To be a slave doesn't mean that he had to live like a slave.

He never stopped operating in his gifting. Joseph was an interpreter of dreams. It was a spiritual gift and operated in him with significant clarity. In the midst of his greatest trials and deepest agonies, he never stopped dreaming and never stopped operating in his spiritual gifting. Others around him greatly benefitted from his willingness to allow God to speak through him. It's easy to become self-absorbed, self-focused and concerned only about your little world when you have been devastated by life and hurt by those who should have been supportive of you. Joseph reached through the hurt, went beyond the personal confusion and made a decision to live out of his spirit as opposed to being controlled by his emotions.

Joseph refused to hold a grudge. If anybody ever had a reason to be spiteful and resentful, it was Joseph. He was taken away from his family, his parents, his home and all that he knew at an early age. He kept his heart pure and at the point that God's plan was unfolded, he was overcome with such emotion that the Bible says he began to weep. The Hebrew word is "Bakah" and the meaning is to cry loudly with great emotions. In fact, the Egyptians, as well as Pharaoh's house, could hear him crying. While his brothers deserved punishment, Joseph extended grace. He could have let them suffer in their drought, but he became the hand of grace that delivered them. Holding on to a grudge is like drinking poison and then expecting the other person to die. Bitterness of the soul affects the one who is bitter to a much greater degree than anybody else. Freedom is only found in forgiveness and moving past the issue. If you don't let the hurt go, it will become the personal prison in which you may die.

What others mean for harm, God will use for good. In responding to his brothers, Joseph actually laid their sin at the feet of the Lord. "Do not be grieved or angry with yourselves, that you sold me as a slave; for God sent me here to preserve life," "So, it was not you that sent me here, but God…" (Genesis 45:5, 8). Many people mistakenly believe that God uses evil to correct or punish or teach His children the lessons that they need to learn. As stated earlier in this book, nothing could be further from the truth. God is always for you and never against you. He doesn't have evil tools in his toolbox and He never stoops to the strategies of the enemy when engaging His children on any level. So, what does Joseph mean in his response to his brothers?

While God certainly did not put it in the hearts of his brothers to betray him, He is always redemptive in every way. He took the evil that was intended for Joseph and used it for his good and for the ultimate good of his family. That's why you can trust God even when things are seemingly falling apart in your life. You can know that even in the darkest hours, God already has a plan to restore you and even as He did with Joseph, He will take you to greater heights than you were before. Joseph's brothers intended to end a life, but God used the evil intent of their heart to save many lives, including their own.

TODAY'S CONFESSION OF VICTORY

Lord, I am so thankful that the days of my life are already in Your hands. I can trust the events of my life to You and know that there is nothing that happens to me that You won't redeem for Your purposes and glory. I set myself today to keep my heart pure no matter what I may face. I refuse to hold people in bondage for what they might do against me, but rather, choose to walk in forgiveness and release. My dreams are not subjective to the actions of others. My visions are not held captive by the opinions or attitudes of others. I will rise to the place of Your calling on my life, regardless of whether I'm in the pit or the palace. I make a commitment to maintain a godly attitude, no matter how vile the actions of others are against me. I believe that the affairs of my life are ordered of the Lord and nothing that the enemy can do will ever circumvent God's purposes from coming into fruition.

Day Seven

SON VERSUS SON

"And the Lord said: "I have surely seen the oppression of My people who are in Egypt, and have heard their cry because of their taskmasters, for I know their sorrows. So I have come down to deliver them out of the hand of the Egyptians, and to bring them up from that land to a good and large land, to a land flowing with milk and honey, to the place of the Canaanites and the Hittites and the Amorites and the Perizzites and the Hivites and the Jebusites. Now therefore, behold, the cry of the children of Israel has come to Me, and I have also seen the oppression with which the Egyptians oppress them. Come now, therefore, and I will send you to Pharaoh that you may bring My people, the children of Israel, out of Egypt."

Exodus 3:7-10

We all know and love the story of Moses. From the very beginning of his life, he was a man marked and set apart by the hand of God. Even at his birth, when Pharaoh was slaughtering Hebrew children, Moses was supernaturally protected from the enemy. Through the divine intervention of God, he was raised in Pharaoh's household as one of his own sons. All the best of Egypt was at his disposal. He was favored, privileged and living the life of royalty. But God had other plans for him. He would be called to give up the luxurious lifestyle to which he had become accustomed, in exchange for a role that would make him the leader of God's people. He would become God's hand and God's mouthpiece in an epic drama that resulted in the deliverance of a nation. God's people had become slaves due to their disobedience, but God raised up a man named Moses to deliver them out of the hand of Pharaoh and to lead them out of Egypt.

Pharaoh was a hard-hearted man with a heavy hand. As an ambitious leader, he depended on the work force of the Hebrew slaves. With a selfish heart and no sense of compassion, he was content to keep them in bondage for his own egotistical purposes. God had other intentions. He opened the eyes of Moses allowing him to see the plight of the Hebrews and began to put a plan in motion that would forever change the life of Moses, the Hebrews and the Egyptians. In response to the brutality that Moses saw, he reacted and killed one of the Egyptian overseers. Now, he's fleeing for his life into the desert, but even that is part of God's plan. In the desert, God not only opens his eyes, but also his heart. He left with a passion, but returned with a plan. The desert can do that to you. What happens next is the legend of heaven. This is more than a battle between brothers, this is an all-out war between heaven and hell. Pharaoh is symbolic of Satan and Moses represents the heart of the Father God towards His children.

The strategy, the timing, the characters, and the outcome are all a part of an epic battle that has been forever recorded in the annals of history and stand as an eternal reminder of the forever faithfulness and covenant of an omnipotent God who passionately loves His children and delivers them from the fierce hand of the enemy.

Lessons of Victory

God strategically led Moses to the desert. In the courts of Pharaoh, Moses was trained in royal etiquette, style, fashion, and strategies of war, diplomacy, government and leadership. The intention of Pharaoh was to engage Moses as a leader in his reign. The years of close supervision and investment would serve useful to Moses, but not as Pharaoh had imagined. God would take advantage of all of the lessons that Moses had learned, but there were some that he would need; that did not and could not come from the house of Pharaoh. To be the leader that would deliver the Hebrews from the strong hand of the Egyptians, Moses would need the lessons of the desert.

In the desert, you have to face yourself. It's in that place of wilderness solitude that you learn what you're really made of. Removed from the accolades of the masses, the comforts of palace life, the pampering of royalty, Moses would have to reach deep inside of himself to discover who he was and what he was about. The whispers of God that are revealed in the desert are often difficult to discern in the noise of normal life, not to mention the noise of palace life. It was in the desert that Moses would learn humility. Out of a heart of brokenness, he came to the end of himself. He was fully thrust upon the provision and care of God and would learn to trust from a place of humility. Pride was instilled deep in the heart and character of Moses and in the desert, he found the real source of power and victory: humility, brokenness and complete dependency upon the Lord.

In the desert, Moses would learn what it is to truly love and fear God. All of the props would be removed, the distractions limited and the stark reality that nothing stood between him and the God of his salvation except for miles and miles of harsh wilderness. With nothing to lean on, the day-to-day lessons of life would become larger than life. The divine connections between the mundane and the miraculous would be invested into a heart and soul that had been emptied by life's circumstances. He was ready. He was a dry sponge, desperately needing the water of heaven to quench his thirsty soul. He was right where God wanted him and where God could download the valuable leadership lessons that he would need in the face-off of his life. It was not a palace-pampered son of Pharaoh that would be able to lead the Hebrew children out of bondage into freedom. It was a desert-trained, wild-eyed warrior who had been emptied of his vainglory and was submitted to the mighty hand of God.

Moses had to see God as bigger than Pharaoh. There is one thing that Moses was quite familiar with: the power of Pharaoh. He had been raised in an environment where the Pharaoh was not only ruler of the land, but considered to be a god. He was worshipped as an all-powerful entity. Moses witnessed firsthand the abilities and accomplishments of Pharaoh. Egypt was revered throughout the known world, and opponents that rose up against them were crushed into oblivion or subjected to slavery, even as the Hebrew's were. If Moses knew anything, it was that he would definitely not accomplish freedom through the strength of the flesh or even by rallying the Hebrews. There was nothing to rally. They were slaves, with years of bondage that had suffocated their passions and dreams and crushed their fighting spirits. Even the strongest warriors among them were held captive by the brutal and unrelenting hand of the Egyptians.

If Moses was going to be successful in his bid to free the Israelites, he had to have a vision that transcended the greatness of Pharaoh. Although God had already intervened in the life of Moses, the only miracle that he had personally witnessed up to this point was the burning bush. He had not seen the strength of God's hand or the fierceness of His heart. He was not aware of the magnitude of God's greatness, nor had he experienced the veracity with which God was able to accomplish His plans and purposes.

Moses came out of the wilderness without a strategy of war. He did not have horses, chariots, armies or an arsenal of weapons at his disposal. However, he did have a purpose and a conviction. He was no longer Pharaoh's puppet, but God's prophet. His heart was set, his vision was focused, and his mind was made up. He was determined and motivated, but not by the carnal ambitions that led him in the early years of his life. He emerged from the desert as God's mouthpiece, God's hand in action and a voice that shook the heavens and earth. Pharaoh was no longer omnipotent. He was no longer the bright and morning star. He was a cruel task-master that held God's people in bondage and for the first time, Moses saw him as the enemy of God's purposes, and he saw God as greater than the Pharaoh. Only now, would he be able to confront Pharaoh with confidence and conviction, knowing that he too, must bow his knee to the God of the universe.

Preparation for Purpose. Looking back is always perfect vision. It's easy to look at where we have been and realize what choices we should have made or paths we should have taken. It's often in the heat of the battle that we lose our focus and forget that this isn't just about a battle; it's about winning a war. We can look at the life of Moses and see that God's hand was upon him in significant ways. Unbeknownst to Moses, he was actually being trained and groomed for the greatest role of his life. To accomplish the task of delivering the children of Israel, Moses would need the lessons of both the palace and the desert.

It's easy to miss the lessons of life that God is teaching us through constant challenges that we face. Within the context of those challenges, we find valuable life lessons that must be learned. It's by surrendering to the heart and hand of the Lord that those lessons become instrumental in shaping us into the leaders God wants us to become.

He would learn to become a shepherd. There is nothing to humble you like giving up royalty and running around after a bunch of stinking sheep. "Now Moses was pasturing the flock of Jethro his father-in-law, the priest of Midian; and he led the flock to the west side of the wilderness and came to Horeb, the mountain of God." (Ex. 3:1-2). A true shepherd is one that will risk his life for the sheep. His safety becomes secondary if the sheep are threatened. On multiple occasions, Moses put his life on the line by daring to confront Pharaoh. That's a shepherd with a heart for his people. As an extension of God's leadership, Moses led Israel as they experienced the rule of God as well as provision and deliverance. It wouldn't be a mighty warrior, a skilled politician, a shrewd strategist, but a true shepherd who understood the heart of God. He was a man who developed a sensitive ear to the voice of God and in humility and patience carried out his commands.

TODAY'S CONFESSION OF VICTORY

Even in my darkest hours, You are always with me. You never leave me nor forsake me. The lessons that I learn in the midnight hour are designed for my blessing and benefit. I trust You to lead me into the desert. I will not harden my heart to Your ways or attempt to outguess You when You direct me into times of leadership lessons. I make a decision today to see You bigger than my mountains. I will not elevate anything or any person above and beyond Your greatness. The strength of the enemy is no match for my God! Your ways are higher than mine, Your thoughts are wiser than mine and Your strength is greater. The greater one dwells on the inside of me and that's enough!

Day Eight

DEAD IN THE WATER

"And Moses said to the people, "Do not be afraid. Stand still, and see the salvation of the LORD, which He will accomplish for you today. For the Egyptians whom you see today, you shall see again no more forever. The LORD will fight for you, and you shall hold your peace."

And the LORD said to Moses, "Why do you cry to Me? Tell the children of Israel to go forward. But lift up your rod, and stretch out your hand over the sea and divide it. And the children of Israel shall go on dry ground through the midst of the sea. And I indeed will harden the hearts of the Egyptians, and they shall follow them. So I will gain honor over Pharaoh and over all his army, his chariots, and his horsemen. Then the Egyptians shall know that I am the LORD, when I have gained honor for Myself over Pharaoh, his chariots, and his horsemen."

Exodus 14:13-18

In his quest for freedom, Moses has now successfully led the children of Israel out of Egypt. In his engagement with Pharaoh he has gained permission to leave a land that was filled with bondage, hopelessness and despair. He has won the battle...at least for now. With over a million people following him, this battle-weary shepherd who has become an unlikely deliverer, is leading a weary and wary people into the desert, but to where? Under the divine instruction of the Lord, they are led directly to the shore of the Red Sea.

Unbeknownst to Moses, Pharaoh's heart has once again filled with rage, anger and bitterness and he has determined to pursue and annihilate the Israelites. He has purposed in his heart to hunt them down and exact revenge on them for the destruction and death that they left in the wake of their sudden departure. Finding them wouldn't be difficult and catching them would be even easier. This rag-tag bunch of broken, defeated and confused Hebrews would be no match for the strength of Pharaoh's army who would be charging forth as trained soldiers on their horses and chariots. Little did they know that while the Hebrews might be easy prey, God had already taken up this battle and their journey would lead them directly to their demise.

Trapped on the shore of the sea, a rumble was heard in the distance. At first, the Israelites could not tell what they were seeing or hearing off in the distance. They were a people that were being supernaturally led by the presence of God in the form of a cloud by day and fire by night. Could the dust, noise and tremors be another manifestation of God's covering and protection over them? It didn't take too long before the heart-wrenching reality set in. The Egyptians were pursuing them, and they had nowhere to go! Word began to spread quickly from the back to the front. Panic, fear and disorder ensued among them as they realized that the Egyptians were closing in on them. They were unprepared to fight and were trapped at the edge of the Red Sea. This had to be the end.

As word of the pursuing Egyptians reached Moses, so did the word of the Lord. God had a plan to deliver the Hebrews, and to end this battle once and for all. What would they do? Divide the ranks? Put what few soldiers they had out front and the women and children behind them? Scatter the masses so that a few just might survive the inevitable slaughter? It would be none of that. God spoke to Moses to stretch his shepherd's staff out over the sea and watch His miraculous and divine intervention.

While fear was rising up in the hearts and minds of the people, something else began to rise up in the heart of a humble shepherd who had now seen the miraculous hand of God on numerous occasions. Faith. He didn't know how, but he didn't have to. Moses had learned to trust God. As he stepped up to the shoreline and in obedience to divine command, he stretched his rod out over the waves. The winds began to blow, the clouds started to gather and the waves moved back in submission to the authority of their Maker. The waters parted and dry land appeared at the bottom of the Red Sea. The Israelites could not believe their eyes! Now, the shout among the masses was of a different nature. Fear, panic and disorder were replaced with amazement, awe and excitement. They weren't going to die after all!

As they began their journey at the bottom of the sea, God held back the Egyptian army long enough to ensure that His people were safely on the other side. In desperation and blind fury, Pharaoh's army followed the Israelites onto the path of dry land. However, this wasn't their miracle, it belonged to the people of God. As the Army ventured into dangerous territory, God released the waves and water and they caved in on the Egyptians, drowning them all. Israel has been delivered, they are safe and the leadership of Moses has been validated. On the other side of the Red Sea, watching in disbelief as their enemies sank under the water, the Israelites broke out in spontaneous song. "I will sing unto the Lord, for He has triumphed gloriously, the horse and rider thrown into the sea.

The Lord my God, my strength and song has now become my victory." (Exodus 15:1).

Lessons of Victory

God's plans are never predicated on your ability to see or understand them. God does not always tell you in advance where you are going, why you are going there, how you will get there or how long it will take. Firstly, he does not have to tell you and secondly, if he did fill you in on all of the details, you would either be filled with disbelief or fear. Had God revealed to the Israelites that his plan included splitting a sea in half, they would never have believed it and would not have let Moses lead them to the edge of it. Many people would mistakenly call this a "blind trust," but in actuality, it is a confident faith that can believe even when not seeing. Moses had heard the word of the Lord and because he responded in obedient faith, he would now see the hand of the Lord. Jesus told his disciples, "Blessed are those who have not seen and yet have believed." (John 20:29).

Grumbling against Leaders only makes things worse. The fear, discontent and murmuring against Moses only served to exacerbate the situation. Fear is contagious. It finds strength in discontentment, confusion and complaining. It spread like wildfire throughout the camp of the Israelites and perpetuated an even greater danger in the face of pending warfare. Moses had earned their trust. He had demonstrated that he could not only hear from the Lord, but was willing to face down Pharaoh on their behalf and was quite capable of winning a show down. God was obviously on his side. You aren't hearing what the leader is hearing, and you're not seeing what they are seeing. Oftentimes, you have not paid the price that they have to be in the place where they are. The choices and decisions that they make are based on information that you don't have. The question is not whether you could do the job better, if you have better methods, more experience, education or ability. The real issue is who the leader is. If you are not in charge, the call is not yours. The decisions do not belong to you and ultimately the outcome is not your responsibility. Your greatest contribution is to support those that are leading the charge. Even in times of disagreement, remember you do not possess all of the information that they do, you have not walked where they have and the ultimate weight of the decision is not on your shoulders.

A dead end is never a dead end where God is concerned. In the economy of God, coming to the end of your rope is one of the best places to be. When you are emptied of all ideas, options and resources, you are finally at a place where you must depend upon the Lord's provision, resources, and wisdom. Throughout the scriptures, we read of stories where individuals have come to the end of themselves, only to find the miracle that they needed. There are lessons found at the dead ends of life that cannot be found anywhere else. In the natural, what looks like the ending of one thing, may just be the very beginning of something even greater. "Most assuredly, I say to you, unless a grain of wheat falls into the ground and dies, it remains alone; but if it dies, it produces much grain." (John 12:24). If you remember, God is the one who resurrects the dead. Give Him your dead end and watch Him perform a miracle on your behalf.

God has a plan for the defeat of your enemy. The Israelites had no idea that God was not only rescuing them, but also had a plan in place to destroy the Egyptians. Many times over in the Bible, God promises His children that He has them covered. "This is what the LORD says to you: 'Do not be afraid or dismayed because of this great multitude, for the battle is not yours, but God's." (2 Chronicles 20:15). As a protective Father, He watches over you with a jealous heart (2 Corinthians 11:2), and surrounds you with His favor, grace and mercy. Your life is not up for grabs and God has promised you that He will always be there for you. "Be strong and courageous. Do not be afraid or terrified because of them; for the LORD your God goes with you; He will never leave you nor forsake you." (Deuteronomy 31:6).

TODAY'S CONFESSION OF VICTORY

Even though I am surrounded on every side, you are my shield and buckler, my strong tower and the one in whom I hide. I thank You Lord that You are not content for me to live my life in slavery and bondage. You sent Jesus to deliver me from the lies of the enemy and a life of sin. The curse of sin has been broken and I now live according to the law of life that is in Christ Jesus. Even when I don't understand what I am going through, or what You are doing, I choose to trust You. I believe that You have a greater plan and purpose for my life and that You lead me into paths that are rich and green and waters that are deep and still. I trust You. I have confidence in You and in Your word. I will not allow my words to betray me or to speak anything other than faith. I will say of the Lord, You are my strength, You are my song, and You are my victory!

Day Nine

MIRACLE ON THE RIVER

"And the LORD said to Joshua, "This day I will begin to exalt you in the sight of all Israel, that they may know that, as I was with Moses, so I will be with you. You shall command the priests who bear the ark of the covenant, saying, 'When you have come to the edge of the water of the Jordan, you shall stand in the Jordan.' " "So it was, when the people set out from their camp to cross over the Jordan, with the priests bearing the ark of the covenant before the people, and as those who bore the ark came to the Jordan, and the feet of the priests who bore the ark dipped in the edge of the water (for the Jordan overflows all its banks during the whole time of harvest), that the waters which came down from upstream stood still, and rose in a heap very far away at Adam, the city that is beside Zaretan. So the waters that went down into the Sea of the Arabah, the Salt Sea, failed, and were cut off; and the people crossed over opposite Jericho. Then the priests who bore the ark of the covenant of the LORD stood firm on dry ground in the midst of the Jordan; and all Israel crossed over on dry ground, until all the people had crossed completely over the Jordan."

Joshua 3:7-8, 14-17

Moses has taken the children of Israel as far as he can. He has come to the end of his life and it's time for a new leader to take up the task, and to wear the mantle of leadership and authority. That role would fall to a young leader who had committed his life to serving Moses and had been groomed in the ways of God. That young leader was Joshua. He had a heart for God and was sovereignly appointed to lead Israel into the promised land of Canaan. As a former slave under Egyptian rule, he was the benefactor of the bold and courageous leadership of Moses. He personally witnessed the hand of God through the life of Moses.

He was an insider and witnessed the most intimate moments in the tent of meeting as well as the response of Moses in the good times and bad. Chosen by the hand of God, revealed by the heart of God and raised up by the Spirit of God, Joshua was a great follower, a leader, a warrior and a visionary. He had a heart to follow the Lord, a head to lead Israel and a spirit to fight the enemy.

His first test of leadership would come in the form of a muddy river. Outside of the flood season, crossing the Jordan was no daunting task, as the river was approximately 10 feet wide and three to six feet deep. However, during the flood season, the river became impassable, swelling to more than five hundred feet wide. Joshua had seen this before under the leadership of Moses, but this test would be personal and would set the standard for a new generation of Israelites. We have a new leader, a new generation of people, a new river, moving into a new land, but the same God! Joshua's challenge would not be the river in front of him, but the head and the heart inside of him. Would he rise to the challenge? Was he the man for the job? Had he learned the lessons well? It was important to God that Joshua be established as the leader, even as Moses was. He gave him specific instructions as he stood on the bank of the only thing separating Israel from the land that had been promised. This time, there would be no Egyptian army breathing down their necks, and no stretching out of the rod over the waters. Joshua was instructed to send the ark into the water first. The priests would carry the Ark of the Covenant into the water, indicating that the presence of God would lead the way in this new season.

As soon as the feet of the priests touched the water, it began to back up to the north, seventeen miles away to a little town named

Adam. Once again, God had made a way for his people. He had provided supernatural passage for them as he welcomed them into the land that he had prepared and provided. In a response of worship, Joshua instructed that one stone be taken from the Jordan for each of the tribes of Israel to erect a memorial on the bank of the river, forever signifying God's faithfulness to a man and his people.

Lessons of Victory

Pay attention in class. As he watched the life of Moses unfold before him, Joshua could never have guessed that the weight of leadership would one day rest squarely on his shoulders. "So it was, whenever Moses went out to the tabernacle, that all the people rose, and each man stood at his tent door and watched Moses until he had gone into the tabernacle. And it came to pass, when Moses entered the tabernacle that the pillar of cloud descended and stood at the door of the tabernacle, and the LORD talked with Moses. All the people saw the pillar of cloud standing at the tabernacle door, and all the people rose and worshiped, each man in his tent door. So the LORD spoke to Moses face to face, as a man speaks to his friend. And he would return to the camp, but his servant Joshua the son of Nun, a young man, did not depart from the tabernacle." (Exodus 33:8-11). There was something happening deep in the heart of Joshua long before he was called up to the big leagues. He was a man committed to the presence of God. He didn't wait until the test was being administered to push in to the heart of God; he was attentive, alert and had a heart that was eager to learn and to grow. Paying attention in class will save you a lot of heartache when it's testing time.

God doesn't always do things the same way. Joshua had a front row seat to one of the greatest miracles in history. He paid careful attention to every detail and it would forever be etched in his mind. Now, he faces a water crossing of his own. Would he stretch out his rod, would he command the river to obey him? There would be none of that. This time he would send the priests bearing the Ark of the Covenant. The waters would not part until their feet touched the river. Two separate bodies of water, two different leaders, two ways to the miraculous, yet the same results. Once again, God showed himself faithful and mighty.

Just because something worked before doesn't mean that it will work again, and it doesn't mean that it's the way God wants it. God reserves the right to show himself strong any way he desires. The key to success is to not attempt to duplicate what God has already done, but to hear the word of the Lord and walk in obedience to his directives in whatever you are facing.

The river backed up to Adam. When the priests who were bearing the Ark of the Covenant stepped into the water, the river began to back up to a little town called Adam. God is doing a new thing in and for Israel, and by backing the waters up to Adam, he is making his redemptive purposes very clear. What is the message here? I am doing a new work in you as a people, and I am redeeming you from all the curses and wickedness of your ancestors. This is a redemptive covenant, and your call into this land of promise is fresh and new. The sin and rebellion of your ancestors does not define you or set the standard for your future. The phrase "guilty by association" is something that we are all familiar with. However, as the redeemed of God, you are no longer under guilt or bondage because of your past. The blood of Jesus has covered you all the way back to your very creation in your mother's womb.

<u>Leave something of who you are, wherever you have been</u>. The Israelites were instructed to build a memorial of 12 stones on the edge of the river, so that future generations would be aware of the mighty thing that God did for their ancestors. "Then Joshua called the twelve men whom he had appointed from the children of Israel, one man from every tribe; and Joshua said to them: "Cross over before the ark of the LORD your God into the midst of the Jordan, and each one of you take up a stone on his shoulder, according to the number of the tribes of the children of Israel, that this may be a sign among you when your children ask in time to come, saying, 'What do these stones mean to you?' (Joshua 4:4-6).

As you read through the Bible, the men and women of God left a mark that cannot be erased. Your life should leave a "wake" that is a blessing to people, not a curse. Future generations should benefit from the godly decisions and godly life that you are living now. Israel followed God right to the river, stepped out in faith, and the generations after them benefitted from their godly choices and lifestyles. Their entry point into the Promised Land came only as a result of their willingness to step out into the deep. God is reminding them to not miss the opportunity to point their children, grandchildren; and those who would come after them towards who He is and the miracle that He performed. Why is that important? Your testimony of the faithfulness and power of God will open the door for the next generation to experience their own miracles.

Your testimony will be an encouragement to believe God for great things in their own lives when they face the impossible. If God will do it for you, He'll do it for them!

God has a perfect plan for my life. He is not content to leave me on the wilderness side of the river. His purposes for me are always yes and amen and include His miraculous, in the land that flows with milk and honey. Even when I find myself in a wilderness situation with no hope in the natural of advancing forward, I commit myself to the presence of God. He is an ever-present help in the time of need and I can trust Him without question or hesitation. I will step forward into the unknown with complete faith and confidence that my God is for me and not against me, and that He will provide all that I need to accomplish His plans and purposes in my life. I am leaving a legacy of faith, hope and love for the generation that is behind me. My children, grandchildren and their children are blessed of God and my life will be used of the Lord to be an example of encouragement and expectation of serving a God who is always faithful!

Day Ten

THE WALLS CAME TUMBLING DOWN

"Now Jericho was securely shut up because of the children of Israel; none went out, and none came in. And the LORD said to Joshua: "See! I have given Jericho into your hand, its king, and the mighty men of valor. You shall march around the city, all you men of war; you shall go all around the city once. This you shall do six days. And seven priests shall bear seven trumpets of rams' horns before the ark. But the seventh day you shall march around the city seven times, and the priests shall blow the trumpets. It shall come to pass, when they make a long blast with the ram's horn, and when you hear the sound of the trumpet that all the people shall shout with a great shout; then the wall of the city will fall down flat. And the people shall go up every man straight before him."

Joshua 6:1-5

Joshua is about to face his first real test of leadership on the battlefield. He has been granted the leadership position held by Moses, and clearly the hand of God exalted him at the edge of the Jordan River. But now, the first city to be conquered looms before them and it just happens to be Jericho. Jericho was not going to go down without a fight. The city was heavily fortified, guarded and protected by fierce warriors. Jericho was "securely shut up" meaning that it was virtually impenetrable. No common, ordinary army would be able to break through its fortified walls. History records Jericho as one of the oldest inhabited cities in the world with the oldest known protective wall in the world. Archaeologists have unearthed remains that date back almost to the very beginning of earth's history.

There was a reason that they survived and prevailed for such a

71

long period of time. What Jericho didn't count on was the strength of the Commander of the Lord's Army. God always has a strategy and a plan that exceeds the wisdom and ability of man and of His enemies. Jericho would be no match for God. If Joshua and Israel would respond to the command and directive of the Lord in humble obedience, they would see the second great intervention of God in Joshua's fledgling leadership over the people of Israel. This would not be a test of Israel's military strength or of Joshua's strategic abilities, but one of absolute trust and confidence in the word of the Lord and their willingness to follow the voice of God even when it made no sense in the natural. The strategy to bring down one of the world's strongest fortresses was contrary to previous war engagements, and had no military precedent. It was critical that Joshua get this one right.

It was critical that Joshua and the Israelites experience victory at Jericho. This was the "gateway fortress" to the land of Canaan. It was large; it was strong and had to be faced by any invading army who had ideas of conquering Canaan. It could not and would not be ignored. It was a city from which great corruption flowed. The inhabitants of Jericho held to pagan beliefs, and the city not only represented strategic importance due to its geographical location, but also of human possibilities. What had been accomplished in Jericho was unheard of in that time and in the natural, Joshua and his army represented no genuine threat. Jericho had withstood these types of armies and attacks many times before.

The difference in this particular attack on Jericho is that is did not originate from the heart of a human leader, but from the heart of the Captain of the Host of the Lord's Army! They would not withstand the advancement of God.

Lessons of Victory

God's directives always trump the standard. As he watched the life of Moses unfold before him, Joshua could never have guessed that the weight of leadership would one day rest squarely on his shoulders. He found himself in the "University of Observation," and the lessons that were imparted to him went beyond the academic. As he observed Moses, he learned humility, patience, obedience and even what it meant not to be obedient. In his servant role to Moses, he was the recipient of spiritual impartation that shaped his heart and his world-view. He had personally witnessed the elements of nature bow down and submit to the word of the Lord and the authority of the prophet of the Lord. If there was anything that Joshua learned, it was that things aren't always as they appear. God's word trumps the lies of the enemy. Faith is greater than fear, obedience unlocks the supernatural and if God is for you, nothing or nobody can be against you.

Things are not always done the same way, every time. He learned very quickly that it didn't have to be the way that Moses did it. What Joshua learned from Moses wasn't about methodology and strategy, but principles and values. It isn't always about the "what or the how," but the "why." Once you settle the "why," the rest becomes nothing more than logistical. Many times in life and ministry, it becomes easy to confuse the what and how, with the why. That's when priorities become skewed and principles become misplaced.

It's not about having a perfect house that is filled with precious treasures that can't be touched or handled, it's about having a home that can be lived in, loved in and where lives can be celebrated and enjoyed. Not one time in the history of Moses and

Joshua was the particular strategy that was given to conquer Jericho, ever employed. Joshua could not lean on past experiences or pull a strategy out of his toolbox. This was a new day, a new season and a new challenge. It demanded that Joshua hear from the Lord accurately and precisely. Many times in the conquest of the Promised Land, it would be imperative that Joshua allow the Lord to speak a fresh word and give leadership for the task that was at hand. God has a "right now" word for you as well. There is nothing for you that is behind you, it's all in front of you and waiting on you to press in to the heart of God and receive His guidance and direction.

The priestly anointing led the way. Make no mistake about it, the "men of war" were engaged in this conflict. They were prepared to fight, they were anxious to fight, but in this particular conquest, they would have to stand down and give way to the leadership of the priestly anointing. Jericho represented the first fruits of many cities that would be conquered by God's people. This strategy clearly demonstrated to the multitudes of Israelites that the battle belongs to the Lord and will ultimately, always be won by the hand and strength of the Lord, not the armies of the flesh.

As the commander of the army, General Joshua would have to step aside and lean not unto his own understanding, his military expertise, or his skill in battle. In fact, chances are strong that if all Joshua had to depend upon was his battle-readiness, Israel might have not conquered Jericho at all. It's been said; "one word from God can change your life forever." So you have a few victories under your belt, you've experienced some successes in life and ministry and you've come a long way. That's great, but what do you do when you're facing a fortified Jericho? A situation that you've never faced before and that looms before you, bigger than life and bigger than your victories and successes? You lean on the priestly anointing. You seek God for favor, for supernatural breakthrough and for a heavenly strategy. The Bible tells us that "the anointing destroys the yoke of bondage." The greater One lives on the inside of you and actually has already addressed the Jericho's that stand before you. God had a plan to defeat Jericho far before Joshua showed up at its gates. Joshua just had to "dial in," get the direction of the Lord and obey. That direction was to depend upon the priestly anointing and the military strength would follow suit. He listened, he obeyed and God's will was perfectly fulfilled.

The shofar and the shout! On the seventh day, following the seventh march around the city, the people responded to the command of the Lord to blow the shofar and to shout unto God. The shofar is a powerful instrument of the Lord that calls people to worship, announces the presence of a king, declares war and assembles the congregation. When the priests blew their shofars, there was a heavenly proclamation of the presence of the Lord God Jehovah! Angels were dispatched and at the word of the Lord, began to push down the walls. There is a time to be quiet and reverent in the presence of the Lord, but there is also a time to shout. There is a time to "be still," but there is also a time to advance and proclaim the command of the Lord. May your voice of praise become the shofar of the Lord as you shout unto the Lord your God! "The kingdom of God suffers violence and the violent take it by force." There are times when you have to stand up and fight, let a righteous and demonstrative anointing fill your mouth and take your stand without compromise. The walls that are before you are coming down in the name of Jesus!

TODAY'S CONFESSION OF VICTORY

As I stand before my Jericho, I take my stand on the Word! I recognize that the walls that loom before me are larger than me, but I also recognize that they pale in comparison to the God I serve and the anointing that resides on the inside of me. I will not walk in fear, but rise up with the shout of the Lord and victoriously declare that "greater is He that is in me, than he that is in the world." My confidence is not in my own strength, my past successes and victories, but that God has gone before me and established me in my coming and in my going. He is the commander of the armies of heaven and angels are at my disposal. I will not cower in fear and intimidation, but in obedience, I march, I hold my tongue and at the word of the Lord I shout! I shout that my Father is exalted, the devil is defeated and Jesus is Lord!

Day Eleven

A SUN UNDER COMMAND

"Then Joshua spoke to the LORD in the day when the LORD delivered up the Amorites before the children of Israel, and he said in the sight of Israel: "Sun, stand still over Gibeon; and Moon, in the Valley of Aijalon."
So the sun stood still, and the moon stopped, till the people had revenge upon their enemies. Is this not written in the Book of Jasher? So the sun stood still in the midst of heaven, and did not hasten to go down for about a whole day. And there has been no day like that, before it or after it, that the LORD heeded the voice of a man; for the LORD fought for Israel. Then Joshua returned, and all Israel with him, to the camp at Gilgal."

Joshua 10:12-15

Joshua is now rising up to a new level of faith, confidence and authority! As he continues his journey of conquest in this new and exciting land that God has given to the people of Israel, the challenges are growing greater and more is at stake. The city of the Gibeonites decided that it would be best to surrender and not take on Joshua and Israel. They are now in alliance with Israel and thus, under their protection and care. But not everyone likes that. Five kings of the Amorites, led by the king of Jerusalem, form an alliance of their own and decide to make war against Gibeon. The only problem is that now it engages Joshua and Israel, and unbeknownst to the Amorite kings, they have bitten off more than they can chew.

The Gibeonites appeal to Joshua, who happens to be in Gilgal at the time. Gilgal is a place that would become a gathering place for prophets. In other words, Joshua was at a place in his life where the word of the Lord was in abundance and unhindered. In fact, when the King of Gibeon cried out to Joshua, the Lord indeed, spoke to Joshua…"*do not fear them, for I have delivered them into your hands, and not a man among them shall stand before you.*" Not only did God birth a word of faith and favor in Joshua's heart, but God took up the battle in His own right. In verse eleven, we find that God sent a great hail storm against them and more died as a result of supernatural warfare than of the battle brought against them by Israel.

The Amorites were a people of the mountains (the high places). Their name literally means to be "proud boasters." They had a confidence in their own abilities, strategies, strength and military might. They amassed a mighty army against Gibeon and Joshua, but Joshua had a word in his heart from the Lord Almighty! When Joshua heard of the attack, he "ascended from Gilgal," which literally means that something in him was roused and he was stirred up. The boasting and threats of the enemy were not enough to deter him from the objective that God had given to him. He gathered the people of war and the mighty men of valor and moved into battle against the Amorites.

In verse nine, we are told that Joshua came upon them "suddenly and all night." Suddenly is the Hebrew word "pith'owm" and it means to surprise. In other words, the enemy did not expect Joshua to be stirred so deeply and attack with such a determined heart and aggressive focus. He is operating at a level of faith that had not been seen before and it's about to result in one of the most amazing miracles ever known to mankind!

The army that aligned against them was the coalition of five kingdoms who were all hell-bent on defeating Joshua, Israel and their new allies, the Gibeonites. This was no small army. In other passages, single armies that came against Joshua could be up to 15,000. In this case, there were five kingdoms aligned against Israel, meaning that there is a possibility that an army of heavily armed and highly trained soldiers numbering 75,000 challenged them. The greatest victory in this story is not that the armies were soundly defeated, but that in order to have the time to finish the job, Joshua literally commanded the sun and the moon to stand still and "God hearkened to the voice of a man" and stopped both the sun and moon in their tracks until Israel had completely won the victory! The bible says that "there had never been a day like that before and there has never been a day like that since!" God not only took up the battle on behalf of Joshua and defeated the enemy by supernatural warfare, but also responded to the command of faith and brought the natural elements into alignment with the word of a man. Imagine the surprise of the Amorites, who were worshippers of both the sun and the moon, when their very "gods" came under the legal authority of their enemy. God not only responded to the faith of His man, but defeated the lies of the enemy of false idol worship.

Lessons of Victory

The greater the level, the greater the devil. While I know that's a worn-out cliché, it's still true. When so much more is at stake, the enemy will align greater forces against you. In this situation, five kingdoms of the demonic came against Joshua at once. In a desperate attempt to bring defeat to the conquest of the people of God, the enemy rallied mass forces, but to no avail. God is never moved by virtue of numbers or the apparent strength of the enemy. The threats, strategies and strength of the enemy are never a match for the power of God. He not only waged supernatural warfare when needed, but also brought the natural elements of creation under the authority of his earthly commander. The key is in the word of the Lord that rested on Joshua. If God is for you, nothing can be against you!

<u>Your victory is not always secured in the realm of the natural</u>. God saw to it that more enemies were defeated in the realm of the supernatural than the natural. Never underestimate how God does, why He does it or when He does it! He has your back and is working on your behalf. Angels have been assigned to you, to your success and no matter how vicious the lies of the enemy are, there are always more for you than against you. You can be confident of God's ability and His working even when you can't see it in the realm of the natural.

<u>Let your spirit get stirred up</u>! The bible tells us that "the kingdom of God allows violence and the violent take it by force" (Matthew 11:12). That simply means to rule and reign with Christ, you must have some spiritual backbone and fortitude. We are not called to back down from the challenges of the enemy! We are not a people of fear, but of great faith and have the word of God over us. His promises to us are yes and amen! God is for us and never against us. We are called to not only guard and protect the realm that is ours, but to conquer and defeat the enemies' lies and strategies and take back the territory that has been stolen from us. We are strong and able, we are more than conquerors through Christ!

The natural world is under your command of faith! When the purposes of God are being challenged, when your world becomes "mis-aligned" by virtue of the attack and lies of the enemy, God will respond to your command of faith, even as He did for Joshua. Joshua spoke in command to the sun and moon. Speak today to the elements of your world, speak today to your physical body, and speak today to situations and circumstances that have gotten out of order. Bring supernatural order to your world. Become a commanding voice of authority. Jesus spoke to the wind and the waves. He commanded that the waves be at peace and that the winds cease. He declared peace to the circumstances and rebuked the tempestuous winds that were being agitated by the demonic. You don't have to settle and subject yourself to the natural or physical elements that are being used of the enemy to torment you or your family. Rise up, take authority over the physical elements and issues in your world that stand in your way and are circumventing the purposes and will of God from fully manifesting in you and through you.

TODAY'S CONFESSION OF VICTORY

I have been called to rule and reign with Christ! I am not just victorious, I am a victor! I am not just a conqueror, I am MORE THAN a conqueror! I am not afraid to stand and face the powers of the enemy. Greater is He that is in me than he that is in the world. The enemies' strategies and strength are no match for the power of God and I have a word of victory on my life. My war is not against flesh and blood and I don't wage war in the realm of the natural. My eyes are open to the realm of the supernatural and I walk in discernment and wisdom. When the enemy aligns forces against me, he is aligning himself against God and the powers of heaven that surround me on every side. I will not back down from the challenges of the enemy and I will not be moved by fear. I am not afraid of the arrows that fly by day or the terrors that come in the night. I am not only anointed to protect the realm of which I have been given responsibility, but to also conquer and take back the territory that the enemy has stolen. I speak to my world and command it to align itself to the purposes and plans of God. I speak to my physical body and command it to come into divine alignment with the promises of health, healing and wholeness, in Jesus' name!

Day Twelve

A MIGHTY MAN OF VALOR

"Now the Angel of the LORD came and sat under the terebinth tree which was in Ophrah, which belonged to Joash the Abiezrite, while his son Gideon threshed wheat in the winepress, in order to hide it from the Midianites. And the Angel of the LORD appeared to him, and said to him, "The LORD is with you, you mighty man of valor!" Gideon said to Him, "O my lord, if the LORD is with us, why then has all this happened to us? And where are all His miracles which our fathers told us about, saying, 'Did not the LORD bring us up from Egypt?' But now the LORD has forsaken us and delivered us into the hands of the Midianites." Then the LORD turned to him and said, "Go in this might of yours, and you shall save Israel from the hand of the Midianites. Have I not sent you?" So he said to Him, "O my Lord, how can I save Israel? Indeed my clan is the weakest in Manasseh, and I am the least in my father's house." And the LORD said to him, "Surely I will be with you, and you shall defeat the Midianites as one man."

Judges 6: 11-16

Here we go, again! Will Israel ever learn their lesson? For that matter, will we ever learn ours? Once again, we find Israel in bondage because of their own rebellion and unwillingness to follow wholeheartedly after the Lord. God gave very clear instructions to them, but their own desires dictated how they lived their lives, what was important to them and the sacrifices they would be willing to make in order to be the people of God. Sound familiar? You and I have a clear directive and mandate in the Word as "to how then should live," but like Israel, so often we slip, falter and make our way back to bondage.

Because of their hard-heartedness, Israel finds themselves in bondage to the Midianites, who were long-term enemies of Israel. Actually, the Midianites were also children of Abraham. After the death of Sarah, Abraham married a woman named Keturah and had six sons by her, Midian being one of them. The Midianites eventually became ensnared into idolatry when they joined forces with the Moabites, and turned against Israel. God told Moses to "treat them as enemies and kill them," even though his own father-in-law was a "priest of Midian." So, in reality, Israel was fighting a battle against their flesh and blood.

The name Midian means strife and that's exactly what they caused in Israel. As a vicious, unrelenting foe, they caused great stress upon the Israelites. For a period of seven years, they regularly consumed every harvest that Israel produced. They killed their livestock and left them in great fear and tread. In response, Israel began to hide in caves that were tucked away in the mountains. In other words, they "ran for the hills." The scriptures use the word "impoverished" which is the Hebrew word "dalal" meaning to be distressed and at the absolutely lowest point in life. You couldn't get any lower than Israel was because of the Midianites.

But things are about to change! Verse eight: "then the Lord sent a prophet!" Thank God for the prophets. Just when Israel had reached their lowest point and were completely laid bare, exposed and had no sense of future or hope, God sent His man with a word in season. God had a strategic plan and that plan (as it always does) involved a man. God had not only raised up a prophet to declare the word of the Lord, but He sent an angel to confirm the word, give specific heavenly tactics and activate the process of deliverance. In addition to the prophet and the angel,

God had also raised up his man who would be a deliverer of the people of Israel...his name was Gideon.

Gideon was born for such a time as this! In fact, his name means "one who cuts down." While we don't know the early history of Gideon, he came to a point in his life where he would have a divine encounter with God and the nation would be saved because of his obedience and the transformation that he allowed to take place in his life and circumstances.

Just like the rest of Israel, Gideon was laying pretty low. He was threshing wheat that would be consumed by the Midianites if they discovered it. To keep the Midianites at bay, he was threshing wheat in the winepress. His response was one of great fear, and while you are supposed to crush grapes in a winepress, fear will often cause you to do things that you are not supposed to do. All of us have done things that we should not have been doing, motivated by emotions that were driven by fear or rejection or sin. Gideon could not have been any lower in his life. He saw himself as fearful, poor and weak. But God saw him differently and God had different plans for him.

In the natural, Gideon didn't have a huge pedigree behind his name. He was from the lowest family in the lowest tribe of Manasseh (which means low, poor and weak), but God uses the weak to confound the wise! While he took inventory of himself in the realm of the natural, God was sizing him up in the spirit and the realm of the supernatural. The angel of the Lord called him a "mighty man of valour." The word valour is the Hebrew word "chayil" and it means wealth, strength, ability and force. The angel was telling Gideon even though you don't see yourself as that, God does and you are somebody to be contended with. God is for you and not against you, He has raised you up for such a time as this and the deliverance of many other people depend on the fact that you can begin to see yourself exactly the way God sees you. Because Gideon responded to the word of the Lord over him, Israel defeated the Midianites and God gave them forty years of freedom and peace!

Lessons of Victory

Rebellion always equals bondage. Old Testament Israel always struggled with walking uprightly before the Lord. We have such a bent towards seeking our own desires and following after the little "gods" of this world. For all of us, it requires a life and heart of discipline, but the key is that our discipline follows our discipleship, not the other way around. You will never discipline your way into the plans and purposes of God if you aren't first a disciple. Falling in love with Jesus and surrendering your whole heart is the source of your power and ability to walk uprightly before Him.

How you see yourself is important! Gideon was never supposed to be afraid of the Midianites and neither are you! He was never supposed to be threshing wheat in a winepress. His perspective of life became skewed because his perspective of himself became skewed. There was an inherent favor on his life, but he had lost touch with that part of who he was. You have to determine BEFORE the battle begins who you are. You have a great promise of life, favor, victory and anointing on you. Your past circumstances, your sins, your failures and your mistakes do not define you. You have been chosen of God, He has raised you up for such a time as this and God needs you to embrace the reality of you, the way He sees you!

TODAY'S CONFESSION OF VICTORY

Today, I run to You! I forsake the ways that have caused me to be separated from You, Lord. I will no longer be defined by my rebellious ways. I will no longer be subject to the strategies of hell that keep me pinned to the past. My past is redeemed by the blood of Jesus; to be remembered no more. If God doesn't remember them, I choose not to remember them either. There is new wine flowing in my life and I am crushing grapes in the winepress and threshing wheat on the threshing floor. In other words, my life is in divine order. I am being raised up by God to bring deliverance to my people. We will hide no longer, we will be oppressed no longer, we are not poor, and we are rich! The enemy has no right to consume that which we sow. We sow in faith, we reap in faith exponentially.

Day Thirteen

TO GLEAN AND GATHER

"So Boaz said to Ruth, "My daughter, listen to me. Don't go and glean in another field and don't go away from here. Stay here with the women who work for me. Watch the field where the men are harvesting, and follow along after the women. I have told the men not to lay a hand on you. And whenever you are thirsty, go and get a drink from the water jars the men have filled."

Ruth 2:8-9

The story of Ruth is not just about "a" woman. In fact, it's about two women. It's a story of tragedy, redemption, restoration and the fulfillment of purpose and destiny in the lives of all who were involved in this amazing tale of God's grace and mercy unfolded. While most of the stories in this book involve wars, strategies, kings and conquerors, this one does not. What links this story to all of the other stories of victory is that, like them, this one involved the divine intervention of God. While researching this book, it occurs to me that every victory is the result of God's divine intervention and the story of Ruth is no different.

The highlight of Ruth's story is that she ends up marrying Boaz, who redeemed her from an uncertain life of poverty and widowhood. However, this was not Ruth's first marriage. She had been married to a man named Chilion, the son of Elimelech and Naomi. In the course of time, tragedy struck the family and in the wake of the death of Elimelech, and his two sons, Chilion and Mahlon, three widows were left to fend for themselves. It would not be uncommon for widows to end up poverty-stricken due to those that preyed upon them. While there were certain guidelines for widows to follow that involved remarriage within the family, it wasn't always as easy as that. Widows could be very vulnerable and at risk for anybody to take advantage of them. In this case, both Naomi and Ruth fell within that area of concern.

Having heard a rumor of provision in the land of Judah, these women made their way to Bethlehem for the purposes of gleaning in the fields, which simply means "picking up the scraps" that were left behind in the process of harvesting. I think you get the picture; a widow who is far from her homeland, no real prospects, no real hope and reduced to gathering scraps on the edge of a field, just hoping to have enough to eat at the end of the day. Little did she know that God was already working on her behalf and arranging circumstances to bring her into her blessing. Little did she know that far before she traveled to a foreign land, God had already set her up for success!

It just "so happened" that the wealthy land owner whose field in which she was gleaning, was a distant relative of her deceased father-in-law. While that may not mean much in today's culture, for Ruth, it paved the way for her to potentially marry again. God had supernaturally brought her to the right place, at the right time to the right person...God is quite good at that actually! It didn't take long for Boaz, (the wealthy landowner) to take notice of her and for her to find favor with him. Once the Lord made the arrangements to bring them together, she did what was required of her to make herself appealing to Boaz and it worked. The word says that he "spread his garment over her" and made her his wife.

God redeemed the life of Ruth and in doing so, also redeemed Naomi, her mother-in-law. He sovereignly directed her steps and arranged provision for her that would have been completely out of her reach in the natural.

You have not been called to be a "gatherer of the scraps!" God's garment of faith, favor, blessing and anointing have already covered you and made arrangements far in advance of where you are right now in life. You may feel like you are on the edge of the field, gathering the leftovers from somebody else's harvest, but let faith arise in your heart, that those conditions are only temporary.

There are two very important aspects of this story that I don't want you to miss. Firstly, notice that Ruth followed the instructions of her wise mother-in-law to make herself attractive. God's favor will see to it that you are drawn and attracted to the blessing, but it is equally important that you are attractive to the blessing. Paying attention to the small details of who you are in life is extremely critical. It is your responsibility to be the very best that you can be and to do the very best that you can do. I've visited churches where the grass was uncut, the building was unclean, the décor was outdated, the style of the service was behind the times, the children's ministry was still using flannel graphs and puppets, the music was sub-par and still using transparencies and then have the pastor ask me why his church wasn't growing! It's simple, you're not attracting the blessing.

The second thing that I want to draw your attention to is that Ruth's family was caught up in the blessing. The overflow of favor in her life poured out onto her mother-in-law. Stop all the fretting and walking in fear when it comes to your family. God has a plan and purpose for you and your family. The generations rising up behind you will discover the outpouring that is the result of you opening up the floodgate. You have a promise of God's favor that includes your entire household. And they said,

"Believe in the Lord Jesus, and you will be saved, you and your household" (Acts 16:31).

Lessons of Victory

You have an appointed season. In the natural, Ruth was done. Her prospects of an awesome life in the natural were dim. Basically, she had "come to the end of her rope." There were no more "ideas," there were no more options, there were no more opportunities that presented themselves. But, God! What Ruth wasn't aware of, is that God had already been working on her behalf. He had already gone into her future and ordained and arranged, not only her provision, but also a complete reversal and restoration of all that was lost to her. You have not been forgotten by God! Even though you may not see the breakthrough in your current circumstances, be assured that God's plan and purpose extends far beyond your current view and He is intentionally drawing you to that which He has provided for you.

God's plan can take you beyond your current borders. Naomi and Ruth were living in the country of Moab, but their blessing was back home in Judah. To get to their blessing, they had to dislodge themselves from the place that they called "home." God had more for them than just a blessing. He also had a people and a place that they would call their own. I remember speaking with a young minister who refused to accept any calling of ministry that was not near his extended family. My instruction to him was that he did not have the right to determine where his ministry would be located. That right belongs to the Lord. He stubbornly rejected my counsel and it wasn't long until he was out of a job, broke and desperate. I reminded him of our conversation and he opened his heart to the possibility that perhaps God had something for him elsewhere and being willing to relocate away from his family was a price he would have to pay. Having made that decision, and submitting to God's leading, an amazing opportunity in an awesome church opened up and they enjoyed a thriving ministry that blessed them, the church and the community to which they relocated.

Don't accept your current status. I've seen many people assume that what they are experiencing in life is simply their "lot in life." Don't buy the lie! Ruth didn't see herself as broken, beat down and defeated. She set herself in pursuit of something greater than where she was, and she was willing to pay the price to get there. Life has a way of labeling you. Your past has a way of labeling you. If you allow your past experiences as well as perceived shortcomings to define who you are and how you see your life, you will never experience the breakthrough that God has for you. Begin to allow the vision of the Word to rise up over you. God has already declared who you are. You are what the Word says you are and you have what the Word says you have. The fulfillment of God's kingdom in you is based on revelation, not observation. We walk by faith, not by sight.

TODAY'S CONFESSION OF VICTORY

God has a plan for me that extends beyond my "status" in life as well as my current circumstances. I am not bound by the tragedies of life, the disappointments of the past or by guilt that is the result of my choices of former sin. Today, I am walking in the fresh revelation of God's purposes for me that will move me into my blessing of life, hope, favor and prosperity. I am coming into my appointed season and my break-though is imminent. The favor of God that is upon me is bringing me into a land that is flowing with milk and honey.

I am NOT a "gatherer of scraps" from somebody else's harvest, but God has raised me up for such a time as this. I am blessed to be a blessing and because of my life, the nations and those that come behind me will "taste and see that the Lord truly is good and gracious."

Day Fourteen

SAMSON: THE MAN, THE MYTH, THE LEGEND

"In those days a man named Manoah from the tribe of Dan lived in the town of Zorah. His wife was unable to become pregnant, and they had no children. The angel of the LORD appeared to Manoah's wife and said, "Even though you have been unable to have children, you will soon become pregnant and give birth to a son. So be careful; you must not drink wine or any other alcoholic drink nor eat any forbidden food. You will become pregnant and give birth to a son, and his hair must never be cut. For he will be dedicated to God as a Nazirite from birth. He will begin to rescue Israel from the Philistines."

Judges 13:2-5

There is a common thread that runs throughout the book of Judges. Following the death of Joshua, the nation of Israel basically forgets who God is and in the process, forget who they are. They abandon the Word of God over them and subsequently fall into idolatry and invite moral and spiritual decline. Their sin and rebellion open the door to invasion by a foreign power; the people cry to God and He raises up a judge to deliver them from their predicament; after peace is established the people become complacent and relapse into idolatry.

One of the judges (or deliverers) that God raised up to rescue His people was a man by the name of Samson. Samson was born to a family that already had all the odds stacked against them. As a part of the nation of Israel, they had been living under bondage to the Philistine nation for the last forty years. Samson was born to a woman who was sterile and unable to bear children. Even the town that they lived in was named Zorah, meaning "the place of wasps." Things weren't looking too great for this family, but they were about to change!

The word of the Lord came to Manoah and his wife that even though she was unable to have children, God would give her a son that would become the deliverer to the nation of Israel. Samson was born under a prophetic promise that he would be greatly used of God and even though the story could certainly have had a different and more preferred ending, he still ended up being included in the Hall of Faith found in the book of Hebrews:

"And what more shall I say? I do not have time to tell about Gideon, Barak, Samson and Jephthah, about David and Samuel and the prophets, who through faith conquered kingdoms, administered justice, and gained what was promised; who shut the mouths of lions, quenched the fury of the flames, and escaped the edge of the sword; whose weakness was turned to strength; and who became powerful in battle and routed foreign armies." (Hebrews 11:32-34).

Samson was a man that even while he had a super strength, he also had a super weakness. If the story of Samson began and ended with him, this would be a sad story, indeed. The good news is that this story isn't really even about Samson, but the fact that God is a covenant-keeping God who forgives and restores and can supernaturally change the "rest of the story." Many leaders (and people in general) have been led astray by their own desires for what has been called, "girls, gold and glory." Samson was pre-ordained by God to be a great leader with a sustained life and leadership that could have served to shape and fashion an entire nation. Notwithstanding, his calling took him places that his character couldn't keep him. He was destined to deliver the

Israelites from the Philistines, but ended up undermining God's purposes by his own unbridled lusts.

As is always the case, the character flaws of this man became the open door that the enemy took advantage of and ultimately caused his demise. *Samson's destiny was deterred by distractions that ultimately became his defeat.* He ended up in a battle for his own life when the true battle was for the life of a nation. He was consumed by passions that were left unchecked and unaccounted for. A life that was prophetically set apart for greatness became a symbol of the ages as representative of the inability to maintain healthy boundaries.

So, how does a man like Samson end up in the "Hall of Faith?" Actually, it wasn't through his life that he gained entrance into this elite assembly. It was through his death. As he comes to the worst moment of his life; blinded, in bondage and a ridicule of the demonic masses, he finally comes to his senses. "Then Samson called to the LORD, saying, "O Lord GOD, remember me, I pray! Strengthen me, I pray, just this once, O God, that I may with one *blow* take vengeance on the Philistines for my two eyes!" And Samson took hold of the two middle pillars which supported the temple, and he braced himself against them, one on his right and the other on his left. Then Samson said, "Let me die with the Philistines!" And he pushed with *all his* might, and the temple fell on the lords and all the people who *were* in it. So the dead that he killed at his death were more than he had killed in his life." (Judges 16:28-30). In this final moment, God's purposes transcended Samson's choices. The grace of God came upon Samson one final time and his life's purpose was unfortunately fulfilled in his death.

Lessons of Victory

The enemy is after your anointing. The anointing is *"the supernatural enablement of God that exceeds your natural capacities."* Samson had a supernatural strength that was the result of the anointing that came upon him. As we have learned, it was undermined and diminished by his lifestyle choices. The enemy wasn't focused on simply ensnaring Samson into the bondages of sin. Certainly, he would long to trap us in sins that beset us, but he is after something much greater in your life, even as he was in Samson's. He's after your anointing. The Bible tells us that sin "separates you from God." "But your iniquities have separated you from your God; and your sins have hidden His face from you, so that He will not hear" (Isaiah 59:2). If he can separate you from God, he will disconnect you from your anointing. Outside of the anointing, you will begin operating by virtue of your own strength. Once that happens, you're done!

Delilah is not always a Woman. Oftentimes, it's assumed that the lesson of Delilah is about being careful with members of the opposite sex. While that is certainly true, we must be aware that Delilah isn't always a woman. "Delilah" represents so much more than that. The lesson to be learned is relative to those things that capture us, hold us in bondage and ultimately steal our lives and our blessing on so many levels. The world has bought into the lie, "if it feels good, do it." Just under the surface of that which seems so appealing and enticing is an addictive spirit that will claw away at your character and integrity and serve to erode your moral and spiritual fortitude. The enemy's strategy and tactic is to entice you with a little, get his foot in the door and then eventually consume and overwhelm you with the very thing that you "thought you could handle." It's been said that sin will "take you further than you want to go, cost you more than you intend to pay, and keep you longer than you want to stay." *Your power over temptation isn't your strength, but your surrender.* Staying in a place of submission to the Word of God and the purposes of God is your only real protection.

A person without self-control is like a city with broken-down walls. That's actually a scripture found in Proverbs 25:28. The point of it is that without a life of discipline and self-control, Satan and his minions have free run of your life. The Christian life doesn't begin with discipline, it begins with discipleship, but living a life that is undisciplined will eventually erode your life of discipleship. Boundaries are a critical component of your success in God. There are certain things that I must not allow, certain places that I must not go and certain doors that I must not walk through. It's not about becoming legalistic, it's about freedom. I have the freedom to choose not to engage in those things that I know will ultimately disconnect me from the anointing and destroy my sense of purpose and destiny before God.

TODAY'S CONFESSION OF VICTORY

I have a prophetic purpose on my life. I was born for such a time as this. This is my season, my time and my destiny will be fulfilled. My past experiences do not factor into the plans that God has ordained for my future. I declare that God has raised me up for greatness and the nations will find deliverance because of the anointing that is on my life. Today, I bring myself into check. I walk in the grace and the freedom to say no! I am not in bondage to the unbridled lusts of my mind nor the culture around me. I have the mind of Christ and therefore; I think the thoughts of Christ, I hold fast to the purposes, the feelings, the intentions and the dignity of Christ in me. I will not be blinded by the deceptive charms of the world, but I see clearly and have the ability to discern the strategies of the enemy. The Greater One lives on the inside of me, and His anointing surpasses that which has been aligned against me.

Day Fifteen

THE CHOOSING OF A KING

"And Samuel said to Jesse, "Are all the young men here?" Then he said, "There remains yet the youngest, and there he is, keeping the sheep." And Samuel said to Jesse, "Send and bring him. For we will not sit down till he comes here." So he sent and brought him in. Now he was ruddy, with bright eyes, and good-looking. And the LORD said, "Arise, anoint him; for this is the one!" Then Samuel took the horn of oil and anointed him in the midst of his brothers; and the Spirit of the LORD came upon David from that day forward. So Samuel arose and went to Ramah."

1 Samuel 16:11-13

The stakes are high. Israel longed for a king and God gave them the desires of their heart. King Saul was chosen of God to lead the nation; but power, politics and prestige changed his heart. Saul lost his focus and God decided to replace him. But with whom? Obviously, it's not easy to replace a king. There was no voting system in place, and the sitting king had absolute power and authority granted to him by God, and recognized by the people as their sovereign. Kings can't just "be replaced" and if so, typically the throne would go to the next in the bloodline.

In this situation, God is realigning His purposes and has a young man in mind that will eventually ascend to the throne. God's desire is to restore His people and bring them back to a place where they walk before Him and serve Him with all of their hearts and lives. Saul has demonstrated that he is not capable of moving beyond the realm of self-interest or leading with a heart that is wholly submitted to God. God is sovereignly directing the heart and life of a prophet who would be instrumental in the choosing of a new king, a dangerous proposition for both the prophet and the one that he chooses. With courage and obedience, Samuel is directed to a sheep farmer by the name of Jesse who had eight sons. God instructs him that among the eight is the next king of Israel. Samuel tells Jesse to bring out all of his sons so that he can get a good look at them and hear the directive of the Lord relative to the future king. Jesse only brings out seven and none of them stir the heart of the prophet.

Upon further pressing, Jesse presents his youngest son, David to the prophet. David had been tending to the sheep and was "forgotten" in the flurry of activity. Once the prophet sees David, he immediately recognizes that this is the young man God has chosen to be the next king of Israel. Samuel anoints him with a flask of oil and sets him apart unto a high and holy purpose. From that day forward, "the Spirit of the Lord came upon David."

Lessons of Victory

David was a man after the heart of God. 1 Samuel 13:14. David was chosen for nobility for a very simple reason, he had a noble heart. That phrase doesn't mean that David was perfect or that he had all of the elements in the natural that prepared him for leadership of this caliber. In fact, quite the opposite was true. David was the very least of his brothers. So much so, that he was overlooked at one of the most important moments in the life of his family. David's heart was unto the Lord in that He learned to trust God and became a worshipper of God.

Do not look on his appearance. The Bible clearly instructs us that we are "to walk by faith, not by sight." (2 Corinthians 5:7). It would have been easy for Samuel to be deceived into believing that any of the other brothers of David were God's choice for king, simply on the basis of their appearance. One of the very important lessons of life is that "things aren't always what they appear." We know that "...Satan transforms himself into an angel of light." (2 Corinthians 11:14). To make the right choice in such an important decision, Samuel had to accurately discern the heart, the mind and the leading of the Lord. In the Old Testament, the Holy Spirit would "come upon" the prophets and leaders, but in the New Testament, we are indwelled by the Holy Spirit and have the ability to operate in the gifts of the Spirit. We can rely upon the gifts of discernment as well as revelation knowledge. We have the ability to discern spirits by the power of the Holy Spirit as He bears witness with our spirit to confirm whether or not something is or is not of God. The gift of discerning of spirits is the anointing to detect the realm of the spirits and their activities. It implies the power of spiritual insight - the supernatural revelation of plans and purposes of the enemy and his forces. It is a gift that protects and guards your Christian life.

The Anointing was for an Appointing...But not Yet! David was anointed as a future king when he was a young shepherd (1 Samuel 16:11-13), perhaps 12-15 years old. He was anointed as King of Israel when he was thirty years old (2 Samuel 5:3). This means that it was at least fifteen years before he became king of Israel. David had an appointed season and so do you. It is tempting to rush out and engage the word of prophecy over your life, but *outside of its appointed season, the anointing is ineffective.* I quite often teach that there is a difference between the calling of God and the sending of God. What happens between the calling and the sending is the "authorization of God." When David was anointed King of Israel, he simply was not ready to serve as king. There would be valuable life lessons in the next fifteen years that would prepare him, test him and ready him beyond his natural capacities. *He was a shepherd who became a king, but he had to grow into his kingly anointing.* Stepping out too early can either circumvent what God desires to do, or it can make the job much more difficult. Being in the right place, at the right time will unlock an anointing that will exceed your natural abilities and will release a supernatural harvest of favor, provision and fruit. Just because the door is open, doesn't mean that you are supposed to go through it, unless it is God who opened it on your behalf.

The Experiences of the Pasture prepared Him for the Palace. Never underestimate the small lessons of life. It was during the times of watching, caring for and nurturing the sheep that David was learning how to become a caretaker of a nation, and wasn't even aware of it. There are many skills that shepherds had to learn in order to effectively care for the sheep. David became skilled at protecting the sheep with his staff and his sling (an art that would later serve to his advantage). He learned how to feed them during all seasons of the year, even when the pastures were bare. Shepherds were known for playing what was called the "shepherd's flute." He would play his flute over the sheep refreshing them and bringing comfort by knowing that their shepherd was nearby. It was through this that David discovered a heart after the Lord and became a man who brought great pleasure to Him. David learned how to care for the sheep during times of special need when circumstances challenged the sheep, when they needed to be protected, when they became sick or wounded and even during the night watches. David was becoming a leader who would have the opportunity to serve in the capacity of king. It was critical that he learn the small lessons well.

God is teaching you big lessons in small ways. Give attention to the details. He is watching your responses, the character of your heart, who you are when there is nobody around but a bunch of sheep. Learn the lessons well, you are being authorized by God to serve Him in ways that you cannot even dream of. Every challenge, every trial, every temptation are all opportunities to prove yourself faithful and to allow your heart to be shaped and fashioned for greater things in your life.

TODAY'S CONFESSION OF VICTORY

I am not forgotten. God knows exactly where I am and what I am doing. There are no unimportant days in my life. I am being shaped and fashioned for the purposes and plans of God that have been on my life, even while I was in my mother's womb. Man may not see me or recognize who I am, but God never misses a thing! I confess today that I will fulfill His dreams for me in my season. My life will be much more than just a long existence, but I will flourish and be fruitful in the courts of my God. I will bear fruit and many will be refreshed because of who I am. I am divinely defended, supernaturally secured, fresh and flourishing in all areas of my life. Like David, I have a heart after God. My heart is easily turned by the Father, and the depth of my longing is to please Him with my lifestyle of worship and obedience. I have an anointing that is opening doors of opportunity for me and I am fruitful in every season of my life.

Day Sixteen

HOW THE MIGHTY HAVE FALLEN

"Then David said to the Philistine, "You come to me with a sword, with a spear, and with a javelin. But I come to you in the name of the LORD of hosts, the God of the armies of Israel, whom you have defied. This day the LORD will deliver you into my hand, and I will strike you and take your head from you. And this day I will give the carcasses of the camp of the Philistines to the birds of the air and the wild beasts of the earth, that all the earth may know that there is a God in Israel. Then all this assembly shall know that the LORD does not save with sword and spear; for the battle is the LORD's, and He will give you into our hands."

So it was, when the Philistine arose and came and drew near to meet David, that David hurried and ran toward the army to meet the Philistine. Then David put his hand in his bag and took out a stone; and he slung it and struck the Philistine in his forehead, so that the stone sank into his forehead, and he fell on his face to the earth. So David prevailed over the Philistine with a sling and a stone, and struck the Philistine and killed him. But there was no sword in the hand of David. Therefore David ran and stood over the Philistine, took his sword and drew it out of its sheath and killed him, and cut off his head with it. And when the Philistines saw that their champion was dead, they fled."

1 Samuel 17: 45-51

The shepherd has been anointed as king and his new anointing is making ways for him, preparing him for the life that is ahead as leader of the nation of Israel. Little did David know that he would be led directly into battle with one of the fiercest warriors that the Philistine army had to offer. Assigned a simple task by his father to take supplies to the frontline on behalf of his brothers, David encountered the Philistine champion taunting and mocking the people of God. In utter disbelief, David could not imagine why this "uncircumcised heathen" was being allowed to defy the God of Israel and get away with it. I love the scripture that says "David left his supplies and ran to the battle!"

When the words of ridicule filled David's ears, the Spirit of God began to fill his heart. David's declaration of defeat to Goliath was not rooted in self-grandiosity, pride or an unrealistic assessment of his own military abilities. When David boasted, he was boasting in the Lord. He had faced down lions and bears and now, in the strength of His God, he would face down a giant. With confidence, he placed a smooth stone in his sling and let it fly! I believe that at that very moment, the angel of the Lord intercepted that stone, gave it supernatural flight and directed it to the exact location where it would bring the bragging giant to his knees. And that's exactly what happened. David's stone found its mark and the battle was over before it even began. The giant made one critical mistake: he overestimated himself and underestimated God's man.

As was the custom of that day, Goliath was the "covenant representative" for the Philistines while David represented the Israelites. Following Goliath's defeat, the Israelites mounted a fierce attack and soundly defeated the army that stood against them and took back all that rightfully belonged to them. The "champion giant" was defeated by a young shepherd whose confidence was not in himself, but in the Lord God of Israel.

Lessons of Victory

Faith Versus Fear. In the natural, David had every reason to be afraid of Goliath. Standing at an impressive 10 feet tall, his upper armor weighed 126 pounds. The head of his spear, just by itself, weighed 15 pounds. This was not a man to be trifled with. Until a simple, God-fearing, young man confronted him, this giant held an entire army at bay with nothing more than his taunts and his appearance. David was not moved at what he saw. He had a history of God's faithfulness and saw the giant as nothing more than an opportunity for God to show Himself faithful as He had so many times before in David's life. You can't walk in faith and fear at the same time. Faith is being absolutely certain of what God has said even when you can't understand it and you don't see it in the natural (Hebrews 11:1). God's promises over you are true, no matter what the enemy has told you. All fear is rooted in the lies and deception of the enemy. If the "giant-issues" that are taunting you and defying what you know to be true, and are causing fear, you can rest assured that it is a battle that has been forged in hell and that battle belongs to the Lord!

<u>The Glory of God</u>. David wasn't concerned about his own reputation or fame. He wasn't worried about what others thought about him. He was jealous for the name of the Lord that was being defiled by the enemy of God. When David stood up, it was as a representative of all that Heaven is on the earth. David was defending more than the nation of Israel; He was righteously posturing himself as an ambassador of the kingdom of God. "Deliver us from the evil one. For Yours is the kingdom and the power and the glory forever." (Matthew 6:13). The enemy has declared his rule and reign over the kingdom of your life and the place that you call community. He has every intention of releasing his demonic strategies of cruelty, bondage and warfare against you and those that are a part of your world. Like David, let warfare anointing rise up in your spirit, stand up in faith and release against him the weapon of praise, intercession and prophetic declaration of who God is, what God says about you and what you say about God!

The Battle Belongs to the Lord. David was the warrior, but this was not his battle. He already knew that should he attempt to defeat the enemy by virtue of his own strength and ability, he would certainly lose. In the natural, David was not big enough, strong enough nor did he possess the military expertise to take on an enemy of this magnitude. The lion isn't the fastest animal in the forest, the cheetah is. He isn't the strongest animal in the forest, the bear is. He isn't the biggest animal in the forest, the elephant is. The difference is that the lion doesn't know that he's not the fastest, strongest or biggest. He has a mindset that he is the king of the jungle and because of that...he is! David had the mentality of a champion. The Bible tells us that "as a man thinks in his heart, so is he." (Proverbs 23:7). Your God is greater, He is bigger, He is stronger and He will never be defeated. It's been said "it's not the size of the man in the fight that matters, but the size of the fight in the man." Make up your mind that your giant will fall!

The Small Things Matter. Far before David was anointed to become king, he was already in the school of the Spirit! As a shepherd, David's heart was being shaped and fashioned to care for helpless sheep but there were much greater lessons that were being applied to his heart. David was learning how to be courageous, dependent upon the Lord and how to walk before God with a heart that was noble, virtuous and easily moved by God. In the pasture, he learned how to protect sheep; in the palace he would become the protector of an entire nation. Under the night stars, David became enthralled with the God of the universe. He learned how to recognize the greatness of God, to worship the

Creator and to rely upon the hand and the heart of God for his daily provision. David wasn't "born" after the heart of God, he *became* a man after God's own heart. David's passions, purposes and character were forged in the crucible of a shepherd's solitude and simple existence.

Your future is now! God is taking advantage of the daily issues of your life to pour into you the gifts that you need to fulfill your destiny. Every challenge is actually the shaping of a champion. Every trial is the foundation of greater things to come. Every test is only a thread in the tapestry that God is weaving. One day it will find its display in the castle of the King as a testimony of your life.

TODAY'S CONFESSION OF VICTORY

I will not cower in the presence of the giants in my life! God has invested into me and given me everything that I need to be successful in life, regardless of the challenges that come against me. I am an ambassador of the kingdom and am well equipped to stand in the anointing of faith and victory. I will not allow the vain taunts and threats of the enemy (no matter how big) to hold me hostage to the slanderous assault of the demonic in any arena of my life or family. I will not walk in fear, but only in faith. The warfare anointing is rising up in my spirit, I stand in faith and release weapons of praise, intercession and prophetic declaration, against the enemies of God. I declare what the word says about me, my family and my community!

Day Seventeen

A JAR AND A JUG

"Then the word of the LORD came to him, saying, "Arise, go to
Zarephath, which belongs to Sidon, and dwell there. See, I have
commanded a widow there to provide for you." So he arose and went to
Zarephath. And when he came to the gate of the city, indeed a widow
was there gathering sticks. And he called to her and said, "Please bring
me a little water in a cup, that I may drink." And as she was going to
get it, he called to her and said, "Please bring me a morsel of bread in
your hand." So she said, "As the LORD your God lives, I do not have
bread, only a handful of flour in a bin, and a little oil in a jar; and see, I
am gathering a couple of sticks that I may go in and prepare it for myself
and my son, that we may eat it, and die."

And Elijah said to her, "Do not fear; go and do as you have said, but
make me a small cake from it first, and bring it to me; and afterward
make some for yourself and your son. For thus says the LORD God of
Israel: 'The bin of flour shall not be used up, nor shall the jar of oil run
dry, until the day the LORD sends rain on the earth.' " So she went away
and did according to the word of Elijah; and she and he and her
household ate for many days. The bin of flour was not used up, nor did
the jar of oil run dry, according to the word of the LORD which He spoke
by Elijah."

1 Kings 17:8-16

There are several dynamics in this story that give us insight into
the life of a major prophet. As the spokesman of God, Elijah
literally finds himself in command of the weather. God is
bringing discipline and correction to the nation of Israel and
through the word of Elijah, is withholding the rain. The

unfortunate aspect of this story is that the prophetic directive is having a negative effect on an innocent widow woman and her son. As Elijah makes his way into a city called Zarephath, he summons this widow lady for nothing more than some bread and water. In the midst of a drought, even a request this small is a major ordeal.

For the prophet, this is business as usual, but for this poor widow, it ends up being a divine intervention in her life that will have repercussions far beyond this particular interaction with the man of God. In her struggle for life itself, she has come to the point where she is facing the prospect of death by starvation for herself and her son. Obviously, she is weighted down by the fact that she has no prospect of provision and has resigned herself to prepare and eat one final meal and then die. What she didn't realize is that she was already under the command of the Lord and He had a plan of supernatural provision for her that went far beyond her natural abilities. "Arise, go to Zarephath, which belongs to Sidon, and dwell there. See, I have commanded a widow there to provide for you." (1 Kings 17:8). She was not forgotten!

There was just one catch to unlocking the bread of heaven. She had to set aside her own needs and focus on somebody else. The prophet was not being selfish in his request. In fact, it really wasn't even about him. He was establishing a principle that would be the key to protection, provision and peace that would fend off the harsh realities of a drought that was caused by the sins of a rebellious nation.

Her Response of Faith unlocked the Transcendent Anointing.
Faith is calling into the realm of the natural that which already
exists in the realm of the unseen. God has already provided for
you. Faith calls those things that "be not as though they
were."(Romans 4:17). That doesn't mean that they don't exist, but
simply that they have not yet manifested in the natural world in
which you live. That's where your faith comes in. God had
already provided for this widow, but her provision needed to be
unlocked and released by virtue of her obedient faith. In this
particular situation, it was mandated that she would follow the
specific instructions as set forth by the prophet and that she
provide for him even before herself and her son. Her inability of
self-provision was transcended by the miraculous provision of
God.

Giving out of your little opens the Door for the Much.
Obviously, this little widow lady didn't have a lot to work with or
a lot to offer. But God doesn't need a lot. In fact, all He needs is
your obedient faith. She only had a handful of flour and a little
oil, and that was more than enough! Throughout the Bible, we see
a common theme of God using only a little to produce abundance.
In the New Testament, God used a little boy's two-piece fish meal
deal to feed approximately 10,000 plus people (Matthew 14:13-21).
But then again, He is the God that created the entirety of the
universe completely out of nothing. Giving of the substance that
you have is the planting of seed, and there is always a harvest
inside of every seed. It's not the size of the seed that's being
planted, but the faith that it is being planted out of. The revelation
of this moment is that you simply cannot out-give God!

Never Underestimate the Unlikely. Elijah was a man on a mission! He was quite familiar with the prophetic and the supernatural. However, that wasn't always the case for those with whom he interacted. There is no evidence that this widow had any special insight into the world of the prophetic, and in fact, this was the first mention of her and even that was relative to what God was doing in Elijah and the nation of Israel. She unwittingly found herself on a stage that was much bigger than the world to which she was accustomed. Very much like God's habit of using a little to provide much, He also uses common, every day, ordinary people to accomplish His will and His purposes. The common thread of those who have been greatly used by God has never been based on anything other than availability and obedience.

Simple faith and surrender are the keys to moving heaven and earth. God quite often "uses the common to confound the mighty" (1 Corinthians 1:27). It's easy to confuse the "flashy" with "faith," but simply put, God isn't impressed!

You Can't Walk in Faith and Fear at the Same Time. If anybody had a reason to be in great fear, it was certainly this little widow woman. Obviously, she had already been through a lot with the death of her husband, she was a single mom and her land was being ravaged by a great drought. It's safe to say that these weren't the best days of her life. Everything at this point in her life was rapidly leading her to a dead end. And then, the great prophet comes into her life. He was about to strip away from her the very little that she was meagerly holding on to. It's interesting to note that among the instructions that God was giving to her, was the mandate to get out of fear. Fear is always based on a lie and opens the door for demonic intrusion and assault. If she was going to follow the prophetic directive, she would have to first deal with the spirit of fear that was leading her to nothing but death. She would not be allowed to operate in fear and neither will you. Faith is your conviction that God can and God will. It comes by submitting and surrendering to the power and the authority of the Word of God. It's different than "believing," it's a "knowing." Faith isn't moved by what you see, think, hear or feel. It's not emotion-based and doesn't fluctuate with the situations or circumstances. Fear will not only lie to you, but will create circumstances that mimic symptoms and bring you to a place where you are absolutely convinced beyond a shadow of a doubt that the worst is about to happen. Faith lays hold of a promise made by God and appropriates that promise without wavering. Fear sees what is and trembles without cause, faith sees what isn't and stands with conviction.

TODAY'S CONFESSION OF VICTORY

My life is represented by the power and the purposes of heaven. Even when I'm not aware of it, I am in partnership with the prophetic course of God's decree over the earth. My life counts and is important. I am valuable in who I am and in what I have, even when it seems to be only a little. God knows how to take the little that I have and create heavenly provision. I choose to put the needs of others first and out of a willing heart, my needs are always supernaturally met. My focus is not on what I don't have but on what I do have! I will not be moved by what I perceive to be lack because I have confidence in God's ability to create a lot out of a little. All that I have belongs to the Lord. My future is in His hands and I stand in faith that I will see the greatness of the Lord prevail in every area of my life.

Day Eighteen

SHOWDOWN ON TOP OF THE MOUNTAIN

"So Obadiah went to meet Ahab and told him; and Ahab went to meet Elijah. When he saw Elijah, he said to him, "Is that you, you troubler of Israel?" "I have not made trouble for Israel," Elijah replied. "But you and your father's family have. You have abandoned the LORD's commands and have followed the Baals. Now summon the people from all over Israel to meet me on Mount Carmel. And bring the four hundred and fifty prophets of Baal and the four hundred prophets of Asherah, who eat at Jezebel's table." So Ahab sent word throughout all Israel and assembled the prophets on Mount Carmel. Elijah went before the people and said, "How long will you waver between two opinions? If the LORD is God, follow him; but if Baal is God, follow him." Elijah said to the prophets of Baal, "Choose one of the bulls and prepare it first, since there are so many of you. Call on the name of your god, but do not light the fire." So they took the bull given them and prepared it.

Then they called on the name of Baal from morning till noon. "Baal, answer us!" they shouted. But there was no response; no one answered. And they danced around the altar they had made. Midday passed, and they continued their frantic prophesying until the time for the evening sacrifice. But there was no response, no one answered, and no one paid attention. At the time of sacrifice, the prophet Elijah stepped forward and prayed: "LORD, the God of Abraham, Isaac and Israel, let it be known today that you are God in Israel and that I am your servant and have done all these things at your command. Answer me, LORD, answer me, so these people will know that you, LORD, are God, and that you are turning their hearts back again."

Then the fire of the LORD fell and burned up the sacrifice, the wood, the stones and the soil, and also licked up the water in the trench. When all the people saw this, they fell prostrate and cried, "The LORD—he is God! The LORD—he is God!" Then Elijah commanded them, "Seize the prophets of Baal. Don't let anyone get away!" They seized them, and Elijah had them brought down to the Kishon Valley and slaughtered there."

1 Kings 18: 16-20, 25-29, 36-40

Elijah is not a happy prophet. Once again, the nation of Israel has turned their back against the Lord and followed after the gods of Babylon. This time, they have become ensnared by the false religion of Ba'al. Ba'al was a god of fertility. Worship of Ba'al involved imitative magic, and the performance of rituals, including sacred prostitution. Ba'al worship was particularly dangerous in that the Israelites included elements of the practice and combined it with worship of Jehovah. To make matters worse, it was encouraged by the wicked king, Ahab, and his wife Jezebel.

Elijah decided that enough was enough and demanded a showdown. He called for the 850 false prophets of Ba'al and Asherah, who was the "mother of Ba'al" and also referred to as the "Queen of Heaven." They would meet at the top of Mt. Carmel and with the heart of a nation at stake, this would be one of the most important moments in Elijah's life. Basically, it was time to "put up or shut up." The entire nation was invited to this epic event, and Elijah would either be vindicated and reclaim a nation back to righteousness or be humiliated before the congregation of Ba'al prophets and worshippers.

The stage was set, the sacrifice was laid out and it's do or die. For an entire day, the false prophets called out to their gods and even cut themselves hoping for a response from the demonic entities that they served. Nothing. Silence. Emptiness. Ba'al has come up short. The false prophets have ended up empty-handed. Now, it is time for God to show Himself strong and mighty through His man, Elijah.

Now it is Elijah's turn. He called on the name of the Lord and the fire of heaven fell in a dramatic fashion. Not only was the sacrifice consumed, but the altar, and even the soil around it. It quickly became obvious that the Lord God Jehovah was sitting on the throne of heaven and ruled over the powers of hell. The false prophets were defeated and now would lose their lives. Elijah had prevailed, but more importantly, Yahweh revealed Himself as the one true God of Israel.

Lessons of Victory

"Christian Compromise" is a tactic birthed in hell. Inclusion is an important aspect of the church of Jesus. Every single person is not only welcome to become a part of the body, but specifically invited! However, we are a people that are "set apart." If you have a pure glass of water, it only takes one drop of poison to pollute the entire glass. A ploy and strategy of the enemy is to compromise the pure message of the word with tradition, other religious beliefs, philosophies and theologies that were never intended to be a part of the gospel message. Culture has embraced various aspects of false religions and many Christians participate in things that unwittingly open the door to the invasion or at the very least, the influence of the demonic.

This isn't about "why can't we all get along?" This is about setting yourself apart unto the Lord God, following the standards of the Word and not compromising who you are, what you believe, or how you live, without apology.

Coram Deo. To live *"Coram Deo"* is to live one's entire life in the presence of God, under the authority of God, to the glory of God. Israel was a covenant people, set apart unto the Lord. Their hearts were turned away and they began to follow after other gods. Elijah was calling them back to who they were. What God has done in your heart is not just for what happens in eternity after you die. You have been redeemed to live a life of victory and purpose here on the earth.

You will never fulfill the life that God intends for you without committing to His presence, His authority and His glory as the rule of your life.

Sometimes We are Called to Confront Hell. We must not be afraid to speak out. Today's culture has created a fear to stand up for what you believe as a Christian. This is intentional on behalf of the enemy. There are times when you are required to "speak up" in order to "stand up." I have had other believers "de-friend" me on Facebook because of a strong position that I took on sin. Their stance was that they didn't want to offend their friends who may be living in that particular sin. The truth is that the gospel is offensive. "As it is written: "Behold, I lay in Zion a stumbling stone and rock of offense, and whoever believes on Him will not be put to shame." (Romans 9:33). The Greek word for offense is "skandalon." It's actually applied to Jesus Christ on many occasions that "His person and career were so contrary to the expectations of the Jews concerning the Messiah that they rejected him and by their obstinacy made shipwreck of their salvation." If we attempt to remove the offense of the cross, we would unwittingly remove the value of the cross. The same sin that is causing the bondage, is the same sin that Jesus died to conquer and forgive. We aren't doing the world any favors by learning to live with their sin and being afraid to confront it. "For the word of the cross is folly to those who are perishing, but to us who are being saved it is the power of God." (1 Corinthians 1:18). The key is that even though the gospel is offensive, we don't have to be. Confronting hell isn't about being an elitist and looking down on people, or judging them. It's about loving people enough to confront their sin and being honest about what the Bible says about it. Your silence and tolerance isn't doing anybody any favors. Had Elijah not stood his ground, the people would never have been delivered from the mocking and insulting power of Ba'al.

God will not be Mocked. God showed up strong on behalf of Elijah, but remember, this was not about Elijah! This was not Elijah's battle, but he was the one who represented what heaven was about and spoke on behalf of God. God does not need to be defended by us. However, He uses people to carry out and execute His will on the earth. We never have to be afraid to speak up on behalf of the kingdom. The Word will never leave you hanging or leave you stranded. God is always faithful to His Word and to carry out His promises. In fact, we are told in the scripture that even though heaven and earth may pass away, His word will abide forever (Matthew 24:35). Many people have a false impression that this is somehow about a great "tug of war" with God on one side and Satan on the other, pulling against us. However, that's actually not the case at all. God reigns supreme overall and everything is underneath Him. He is never on the same equal footing as Satan and neither are you; he is under your feet as well. God showed Himself faithful to Elijah and He always will. We are told in Jeremiah that God "watches over His Word to perform it and make sure that it is fulfilled." (Jeremiah 1:12).

The battle does not belong to me, but I am called of God to fight the good fight of faith! Today I declare that I will not bow or cower in the face or threats of the enemy against myself; my family, or my destiny. The powers of hell cannot stand against the Word of the Lord. Greater is He that is in me than He that is in the world. I will not compromise who I am, what I believe, how I live or who I am becoming. I stand on the mountain and decree the sovereignty of God over my world. I confront the powers of darkness in faith and in the strength and power of the Word. My God is mighty, my God is awesome, my God rules and reigns over all the earth!

Day Nineteen

A DIRTY DIP

"Then Naaman went with his horses and chariot, and he stood at the door of Elisha's house. And Elisha sent a messenger to him, saying, "Go and wash in the Jordan seven times, and your flesh shall be restored to you, and you shall be clean." But Naaman became furious, and went away and said, "Indeed, I said to myself, 'He will surely come out to me, and stand and call on the name of the LORD his God, and wave his hand over the place, and heal the leprosy.' Are not the Abanah and the Pharpar, the rivers of Damascus, better than all the waters of Israel? Could I not wash in them and be clean?" So he turned and went away in a rage. And his servants came near and spoke to him, and said, "My father, if the prophet had told you to do something great, would you not have done it? How much more then, when he says to you, 'Wash, and be clean'?" So he went down and dipped seven times in the Jordan, according to the saying of the man of God; and his flesh was restored like the flesh of a little child, and he was clean."

2 Kings 5:9-14

The focal point of this amazing story is actually a high-ranking commander in the Syrian army. Naaman was a powerful man. He was powerful in that he had an entire Army at his disposal, powerful because he had the respect and admiration of the King, and powerful because he was a mighty man of valor. Unfortunately, he was also a leper. The leprosy of Naaman was most likely not the leprosy that you and I know of today or that was prominently mentioned in the New Testament. Scholars agree that it was probably a serious skin issue, and a disease that Naaman desperately wanted to be healed of. Years of doctors, treatments and lots of money, were all to no avail. Naaman had the world by the tail, but could not find a solution to the very thing that plagued him.

Through the word of a young, slave girl, Naaman's life was about to change forever, but first his heart would have to change. Hearing of the prophet, Elisha, Naaman made his way to Israel, seeking that which had eluded him for so long. He found his way to Elisha's house, but it wasn't going to be as easy as that! The prophet was challenging something greater in Naaman's heart and that was an issue of pride. He released the command of healing over the veteran warrior, but it would come with a price. Naaman would have to dip in the Jordan River seven times to receive his cleansing.

The Jordan River was by no means a resort place to hang out with your friends. It was a murky, muddy and often polluted river to be avoided at all costs. A man of Naaman's stature would never choose to bathe in a nasty river like the Jordan and he found offense that the prophet instructed him to do so. At the wise encouragement of one of his servants, he eventually determined that he had nothing to lose and followed the word of the prophet. After submerging himself seven times as instructed, his skin became clear, and he was completely healed of his leprosy. In great joy and thanksgiving, he offered Elisha one million dollars in today's currency. Elisha refused the offer, and in the process, Naaman's heart was turned to the Lord God of Israel.

Lessons of Victory

Your testimony can make a difference. The testimony of a young servant girl became the very thing that engaged the kings of two different countries and ultimately brought healing to her master. Had she not revealed that there was a prophet in Israel, this would not even be a story that we would be aware of today. We are God's ambassadors and the testimony of your life is exactly what people need to hear! You don't have to be a theologian or a learned scholar of the Bible. All you need is to speak up and be strong in your witness of what God has done in your life. You are a living, walking, breathing testimony of the goodness and greatness of God. One word from God through your testimony can change somebody's life forever!

You can't buy what God wants to do in your life. Elisha had a heart of integrity and would not run the risk of allowing the gifts of God or the power of God to be seen as something for sell. Elisha's refusal to accept Naaman's gift further enforced the message to him that it was not by power or might that he had been healed, but only by the hand of the Lord. Naaman would always remember that he had freely received the miracle that he needed and that he had nothing personal at stake other than his obedience and submission to the word of the prophet. The message to us today is that God is not impressed with the material goods that you might possess. God is not moved because of your riches and you cannot give your way into the kingdom of God or into the favor of the King. "Freely you have received, freely give." (Matthew 10:8).

You must humble yourself to receive. Naaman never anticipated that he would have to humble himself at the word of the prophet and dip into a dirty river in order to receive what God had for him. Proverbs 11:2 says that "when pride comes, then comes disgrace, but with the humble is wisdom." Pride in our life can block the activation of God's blessing and the fullness of all that He wants to do in your life. One definition of pride is "to have a high opinion of your own dignity, importance, merit, or superiority." Pride leads to excessive self-esteem and conceitedness. True humility is seeing yourself exactly the way God sees you, but not elevating yourself above who God has called you to be. God wants you to see yourself as blessed, anointed, highly favored and overcoming. But none of those things are because of your own ability or your own worth. Jesus paid the price for who you are and it's only by virtue of His accomplishments on the cross that you have anything in your life of eternal worth.

Healing wasn't found in the River, but in Obedience. Elisha was basically challenging Naaman. As a prophet, he had an insight into the struggles and condition of Naaman's heart. The truth is that Elisha gave him a gift other than the miracle of healing. He brought divine correction to his character and Naaman left a man who emerged from the dirty river not only healed, but also whole. This divine encounter with the prophet of God addressed Naaman's life: spirit, soul and body. Your obedience to the Word of God opens the door for God to release in you His full provision. In fact, your obedience is called "faith." It's your faith that unlocks the miraculous, and brings all that God has purposed and planned for your life into fruition.

TODAY'S CONFESSION OF VICTORY

Lord, baptize me with the cleansing water of Your word! I will not find myself submerged in the waters of pride or vanity, but willingly submit to the voice of the Great Shepherd and drink from the well of living water that comes only from Him. I often find myself covered with the leprosy of my own sin and the residue of the sinful world in which I live. Even though the world does not understand the water of the Word, I find life, healing, health and wholeness as I obey the Word of the Lord over me. Today, it is my confession and declaration that I am the healed of God and I will never be sick another day in my life. I will not allow my pride to hold me back from all that God has for me. I humble myself in the sight of the Lord and in my humility, He lifts me up and sets my feet on the high places, where I rule and reign with Him.

Day Twenty

A FISHY STORY

*"Now the word of the LORD came to Jonah the son of Amittai, saying,
"Arise, go to Nineveh, that great city, and cry out against it; for their
wickedness has come up before Me." But Jonah arose to flee to Tarshish
from the presence of the LORD. He went down to Joppa, and found a ship
going to Tarshish; so he paid the fare, and went down into it, to go with
them to Tarshish from the presence of the LORD. But the LORD sent out
a great wind on the sea, and there was a mighty tempest on the sea, so
that the ship was about to be broken up. Then the mariners were afraid;
and every man cried out to his god, and threw the cargo that was in the
ship into the sea, to lighten the load. But Jonah had gone down into the
lowest parts of the ship, had lain down, and was fast asleep. Then the
men were exceedingly afraid, and said to him, "Why have you done
this?" For the men knew that he fled from the presence of the LORD,
because he had told them. Then they said to him, "What shall we do to
you that the sea may be calm for us?"—for the sea was growing more
tempestuous. And he said to them, "Pick me up and throw me into the
sea; then the sea will become calm for you. For I know that this great
tempest is because of me." So they picked up Jonah and threw him into
the sea, and the sea ceased from its raging. Then the men feared the
LORD exceedingly, and offered a sacrifice to the LORD and took vows.
Now the LORD had prepared a great fish to swallow Jonah. And Jonah
was in the belly of the fish three days and three nights."*

Jonah 1:1-5, 10-12, 15-17

Jonah was a prophet of the Lord that was given a special
assignment as a missionary. Nineveh was one of the largest
Mediterranean cities of the time and the people were extremely
evil. So much in fact, that God had decided to completely destroy

them. In His mercy, He spoke to the prophet Jonah to travel to the city with a warning and a call to repentance. Jonah wasn't too thrilled with the prospect of going to Nineveh, because of the chance that they would indeed repent and would be spared the wrath of God. Nineveh was a bitter enemy of Israel and if they were spared, they would continue being a major threat to the people of Israel. Jonah would just as soon have seen them annihilated.

Instead of going to Nineveh as God commanded, Jonah decided to get on a ship and go to a town across the Mediterranean Sea called Tarshish. Jonah had no particular interest in this town, except for the fact that merchant ships were sailing there and it would be an easy way for him to get away from his responsibility to call Nineveh to repentance. Or would it? Running away from his prophetic assignment wouldn't be as easy as it seemed. Jonah assumed that he could take an innocent trip across the sea and all of his problems would be solved and God would release him from his call. Nothing would be further from the truth.

In the middle of the Mediterranean Sea, the storm became so great that the merchant sailors were afraid for their lives. Jonah knew that he was the cause of the storm and talked the sailors into throwing him overboard. We know the rest of the story, but this actually points to the fact that Jonah had come to the end of his rope, is suicidal and willing to end his own life. However, God had other plans! Sinking in the sea, God sent a giant fish to actually swallow Jonah and he spent the next three days and nights in the belly of that fish. I am going to guess that he is in a place where he now is repenting of his own sins and is willing to do whatever God has called him to do, even if he doesn't agree with it.

After a torturous three days and nights on the inside of a giant fish, God commands the fish to vomit him on dry land. I'm not sure that I would have wanted to see that spectacle, but I can imagine it. Bleached a ghostly white from the acids in the fish's belly, covered in fish slime, drenched in vomit, Jonah is a sight to behold! He is a mess, but he is now ready to head to Nineveh. Once he gets there, he preaches exactly what God dictates and sure enough, the people of Nineveh repent and the entire city is spared the wrath of God.

Lessons of Victory

God reigns Supreme over All the Nations. The very last thing that Jonah wanted or expected was that a sworn enemy of Israel would be given the chance to repent of their sins and be spared the wrath of God. Nineveh was the capital of the Assyrian empire. The Assyrians were particularly brutal and cruel, even known for skinning their captives alive. The prophet Nahum describes them as "lions, tearing and feeding on the nations" (Nahum 2:11-13). As an Israelite, Jonah had every right to wish that this ferocious people who constantly attacked Israel would be wiped out. But that wasn't Jonah's call. God is sovereign and He deals with the nations according to His pleasures and purposes, not ours. Jonah's responsibility (as is ours), is to obey God and declare His word over all the nations, or shall I say nationalities? God is the Lord over all the nations and there is no place for ethnic pride in the kingdom. Far before we are citizens of any particular country, or of any particular race or tribe, we are citizens of the kingdom of God. Our allegiance, first and foremost is to the Lord!

We must obey God even when the circumstances are Contrary to our Hopes and Expectations. God is infinite, but we are finite. He sees the beginning from the end, but we see through a glass darkly (1 Corinthians 13:12). God always has an eternal perspective and knows the outcome of any given situation before it even occurs. In our limited knowledge, understanding and experience, we are safe when we trust God, obey Him and leave the results to His wisdom. What we do know is that God only operates from the perspective of love. Even when we don't understand the "why" and even the "what," we can always trust the "Who." The ways of the Lord, the timing of the Lord and even the perspective of the Lord are much higher than our own. We have to know that even if we don't have a human understanding about what we are going through and don't see reasoning in the natural, we are called to walk by faith and not by sight. We can trust Him in the darkest of nights and know that He has already ordained the breaking of the dawn over the situations and circumstances of our lives if we will but trust Him.

God Uses us despite Ourselves. Jonah was a man on the run. He was full of insecurities and fear and tried to take things into his own hands. God was exhibiting a gracious and forgiving spirit towards the people of Nineveh, but Jonah was bitter, revengeful and saw this as an opportunity to defeat his enemies. Trying to run away from the prophetic call of the Lord was the least of Jonah's worries. He was now operating out of fear and running in disobedience. As we find in so many biblical narratives, both fear and disobedience opens the door to becoming vulnerable to the exploits of the enemy. In Jonah's case, his disobedience opened the mouth of a giant fish! In spite of the fact that Jonah decided to take matters into his own hands, God still chose to use him. He would have to humble him and bring back to a place of understanding and obedience, but notwithstanding, Jonah was still God's man. God could have easily allowed Jonah to perish in the waves of the Mediterranean, but He showed Him the same level of grace and mercy that He wanted to show to the people of Nineveh. God doesn't look at your weaknesses and reject you from being used by Him. He doesn't choose somebody else because they are more talented than you or have a greater skill set or higher education than you. As it was in Jonah's case, God was working out some character flaws in His chosen man. The people of Nineveh were spared, but so was the prophet. The people of Nineveh experienced the loving grace and mercy of God, but so did the runaway man of God. God is longing to use you for His purposes, plans and passions, but you don't have to be perfect in order for Him to do so. Your greatest ability is always your willingness and your availability!

God doesn't want to Judge You, He wants to Forgive You. The heart of God is that all people would come to a saving knowledge of Him as their Father. God is not interested in judging you for your sins, punishing you because of your sins, or condemning you in your sins. God loves you and wants to forgive you, cleanse you and restore you. Psalm 103:12 says that "as far as the east is from the west, so far does he remove our transgressions from us." In fact, what God desires is that we judge our own sins. How do you do that? You judge your sin by virtue of acknowledgement, confession and repentance and asking forgiveness. Once you do that, you enable God to forgive you on the basis of the shed blood of Jesus Christ. God didn't want to condemn and destroy Nineveh. He sent His prophet to them for the very purpose of forgiving and restoring them. God loves the sinner. He doesn't compromise or tolerate the sin, but that doesn't change the fact that He loves the whole world and sent His son, Jesus Christ to die for those who are dying in their own sins.

TODAY'S CONFESSION OF VICTORY

Many times in my life, I have been a "dead man running." I have attempted to do life my own way, to work out my plans and purposes without even consulting the Father. I ask you to forgive me Lord for pursuing my own passions without a thought of your will or intentions for my life. As an ambassador of Christ, I operate in divine love and supernatural calling. I see the lost, I have a heart for those that don't know God and I am equipped to proclaim the good news of the gospel. My life counts and makes a difference. People see my life and are made aware of the goodness of God that operates in me and through me. I was born for such a time as this, not only to my family, but to the nations. Many will taste and see that the Lord is good because of who I am in God!

Day Twenty One

A VALLEY OF DRY BONES

*"The hand of the LORD came upon me and brought me out in the Spirit
of the LORD, and set me down in the midst of the valley; and it was full
of bones. Then He caused me to pass by them all around, and behold,
there were very many in the open valley; and indeed they were very dry.
And He said to me, "Son of man, can these bones live?"*

So I answered, "O Lord GOD, You know."

*Again He said to me, "Prophesy to these bones, and say to them, 'O dry
bones, hear the word of the LORD! Thus says the Lord GOD to these
bones: "Surely I will cause breath to enter into you, and you shall live. I
will put sinews on you and bring flesh upon you, cover you with skin
and put breath in you; and you shall live. Then you shall know that I am
the LORD." So I prophesied as I was commanded; and as I prophesied,
there was a noise, and suddenly a rattling; and the bones came together,
bone to bone. Indeed, as I looked, the sinews and the flesh came upon
them, and the skin covered them over; but there was no breath in them.*

*Also He said to me, "Prophesy to the breath, prophesy, son of man, and
say to the breath, 'Thus says the Lord GOD: "Come from the four winds,
O breath, and breathe on these slain, that they may live." ' " So I
prophesied as He commanded me, and breath came into them, and they
lived, and stood upon their feet, an exceedingly great army.*

*Then He said to me, "Son of man, these bones are the whole house of
Israel. They indeed say, 'Our bones are dry, our hope is lost, and we
ourselves are cut off!' Therefore prophesy and say to them, 'Thus says
the Lord GOD: "Behold, O My people, I will open your graves and cause
you to come up from your graves, and bring you into the land of Israel.
Then you shall know that I am the LORD, when I have opened your*

graves, O My people, and brought you up from your graves. I will put My Spirit in you, and you shall live, and I will place you in your own land. Then you shall know that I, the LORD, have spoken it and performed it," says the LORD. "

Ezekiel 37:1-14

By the hand of the Lord, the prophet Ezekiel finds himself in Death Valley. He is literally in one of the lowest spots on the face of the earth. As the site of the former Sodom and Gomorrah, the valley that Ezekiel is in 1,300 feet below sea level. He really is at the bottom of the earth. Although this was a vision, the scene that unfolded before the prophet was actually one that was quite real in those days. Armies would win a great victory and would leave thousands of slain enemies that would become skeletons and reflect the very thing that Ezekiel was seeing in this vision.

Ezekiel was not only a prophet, but he was also a priest. The Lord set him in the midst of this valley where it would have been strictly forbidden for him to have any contact with dead bodies. He would have been very nervous and very uncomfortable being in this gruesome field of death, yet God was subjecting him to this vision for a very specific purpose. The dry bones represented the nation of Israel that had forsaken God and became lifeless and dead in their relationship with Yahweh.

These dry bones represented the hopelessness that Israel had come to. These were people that once lived fruitful, productive and very real lives. They represented dreams that had died, futures that were never realized and a potential that was never fulfilled. As the prophet walked among the mass of skeletal remains, he was challenged as to whether or not these bones could ever live again. Obviously without a supernatural, divine intervention, these bones would lay there untouched and continuing to decay without any hope.

Ezekiel was instructed to prophesy and decree the word of the Lord to that which had crossed into the impossible in the realm of the natural. These skeletons went beyond a dead body. They came to the place where there was nothing to work with any longer. They had been the prize for vultures and animals that gouged themselves on their flesh. It was only a matter of time before even the skeletons themselves would become non-existent.

At the word of the Lord, Ezekiel began to prophesy life and restoration and the breath of God began to blow upon that which was lifeless, hopeless and forgotten. The bones began to shake, they began to move, and they began to supernaturally posture themselves into a form and fashion that could sustain life. While flesh, muscle and skin came upon these bones, they remained lifeless. As Ezekiel continued to prophesy, the breath of God in the form of the four winds of the earth began to fill the lifeless bodies. Breath came into them, and they came alive and began to rise as a mighty army unto the Lord.

Ezekiel was prophesying to the people of God. Those that had lost their vision, their passion, purpose and sense of divine destiny would rise up with new hope and a sense of belonging to the Lord God of Israel as a mighty and strong people. In this amazing vision, God demonstrates to the prophet that He is not only passionate and purposeful in restoring the land of Israel, but His people unto Himself!

Lessons of Victory

<u>**God is Committed to Your Restoration**</u>. We have all found

ourselves in times and places where we don't even recognize where we are and often, who we are. Choices, decisions and circumstances can bring us to a place in life where we discover that we are empty, lacking and wanting. Jesus said in Matthew 11:28-29, "Come to Me, all you who labor and are heavy laden, and I will give you rest." Jesus is actually talking to two different groups of people in this verse. Firstly, He is talking to those who are basically just worn out from life. The labors of life have become heavy and burdensome and a break is desperately needed. Secondly, He is talking to those who have become the subject of somebody else's decision. To be "heavy laden" is to be under the weight of the actions of other people. In both of these situations, He is promising rest that only comes from His presence. The Greek word for rest in this verse is in the context of recovery and restoration. The Father is committed to restoring everything that you have lost, whether by virtue of our own decisions or those of others. "I will restore the years that the locust has eaten." (Joel 2:25).

I set before you Life and Death...choose Life! The Bible tells us that God sets before us life and death and encourages us to choose life (Deuteronomy 30:19). At the word of the Lord, it was the responsibility of the prophet to begin declaring life even when he was surrounded by death. In the midst of a hopeless valley filled with despair, he would have to step out in faith and not be moved by what he was seeing in the natural. Life and death is in the power of the tongue (Proverbs 18:21). Every single day, you and I are faced with the options of life or death. We are called out of darkness and into the light and we are people of life. Speak life, decree life, and live life to its fullest and engage the anointing of life. God wants you to live healthy, happy and whole and to live a long, healthy, blessed, prosperous life on the earth that brings

Him glory and honor. Choose life today!

It's Never Too Late. I've often heard people say that "if only they were younger," or "if they could get those years back." I certainly understand what they are saying, but look at the miracle in this vision that God brought to Ezekiel. In essence, God was saying that no matter how desperate the situation may become, no matter how hopeless it may seem, it's never too late. We are told in the scriptures that "and we all, with unveiled face, beholding the glory of the Lord, are being transformed into the same image from one degree of glory to another. For this comes from the Lord who is the Spirit." What that scripture means; is that your best days are still ahead of you. You may have made a mess of your life, you may not have made the best decisions or had the best results from a life that was lived outside of God's will, but it's never too late to return to the Lord. These bones had gone well beyond hope in the natural. They were not only dead, but were decaying. If God can breathe life into a valley full of skeletal remains and raise up a mighty army, He can breathe life back into you and raise you up for His purposes and for a destiny that only He can fulfill.

Calling Things that Be Not as though they Were. When we see lack, God sees fullness. When we hear failure, God hears success. When we are afraid, God fills us with boldness and confidence. It's easy to "call those things that are, as though they are not," but that's not what we are biblically instructed to do. We are told to "call those things that be not as though they were." (Romans 4:17). Ezekiel spoke life where there was no life. He prophesied the wind where there was no wind. The prophet declared and decreed the word of the Lord to bones that had no way of hearing him, but his declaration was spoken into the heavenlies. As he began to speak the will and the Word of the Lord, the release of heaven started manifesting. "Now faith is the substance of things hoped for, the evidence of things not seen." (Hebrews 11:1). You don't have to see it to believe it. It doesn't have to be tangible in order for it to be real. Step out in faith and begin to say what the Word says, begin to believe for that which hasn't even manifested yet in the natural. Ezekiel was speaking life to the dead and God honored his faith. He will honor yours as well.

An Army in the Making. That little boy that is not paying attention in Sunday class...he may be your next pastor. That girl that cannot seem to get it all together, she may be a world-class doctor one day. That youth group that seems disinterested and only concerned about having a good time, they may be the very catalyst that God uses to bring revival to your city. The bones of this valley were a big mess. The prophet had no reason to believe that what he was seeing had the potential of becoming a mighty army unto the Lord. But God sees things differently. God doesn't look at you in terms of who you used to be, He sees you for who you are yet to become. God sees your potential and we need to see the potential in others. We have heard that we shouldn't judge a book by its cover, but that means that you are going to have to dig a little deeper and discover hidden treasures in people that others may miss. God is a God of the second chances, and He can take brokenness and make it whole in an instant. He can release the breath of His word and cause life to come into a bruised, wounded vessel and raise up a mighty man or woman of valor.

Even though I walk through the valley of the shadow of death, I will fear no evil. I am not moved by what I see, hear, think or feel. Even though I may look around my life and see death, decay and dreams that have been lost, my life is not over. My best days are ahead of me and God has a future and a hope for me. I will walk in the spirit of revival and restoration. I bring my broken and shattered dreams to the Lord and I allow the breath of His word to wash over my disappointments, my failures and my dreams that have been lost. Today, I choose life. Today, I rise up in faith and call those things that be not as though they were. I have a promise over my life and I will not believe or accept the lie that I can never be used mightily of the Lord. I have great worth and value to my King, and I step into the blessing and promise of who I am in Him.

Day Twenty Two

THREE HEBREW CHILDREN

"Therefore at that time certain Chaldeans came forward and accused the Jews. They spoke and said to King Nebuchadnezzar, "O king, live forever! You, O king, have made a decree that everyone who hears the sound of the horn, flute, harp, lyre, and psaltery, in symphony with all kinds of music, shall fall down and worship the gold image; and whoever does not fall down and worship shall be cast into the midst of a burning fiery furnace. There are certain Jews whom you have set over the affairs of the province of Babylon: Shadrach, Meshach, and Abed-Nego; these men, O king, have not paid due regard to you. They do not serve your gods or worship the gold image which you have set up."

Then Nebuchadnezzar, in rage and fury, gave the command to bring Shadrach, Meshach, and Abed-Nego. So they brought these men before the king. Nebuchadnezzar spoke, saying to them, "Is it true, Shadrach, Meshach, and Abed-Nego, that you do not serve my gods or worship the gold image which I have set up? Now if you are ready at the time you hear the sound of the horn, flute, harp, lyre, and psaltery, in symphony with all kinds of music, and you fall down and worship the image which I have made, good! But if you do not worship, you shall be cast immediately into the midst of a burning fiery furnace. And who is the god who will deliver you from my hands?"

Shadrach, Meshach, and Abed-Nego answered and said to the king, "O Nebuchadnezzar, we have no need to answer you in this matter. If that is the case, our God whom we serve is able to deliver us from the burning fiery furnace, and He will deliver us from your hand, O king. But if not, let it be known to you, O king, that we do not serve your gods, nor will we worship the gold image which you have set up." Then Nebuchadnezzar was full of fury, and the expression on his face changed toward Shadrach, Meshach, and Abed-Nego. He spoke and commanded that they heat the furnace seven times more than it was usually heated. And he commanded certain mighty men of valor who were in his army to bind Shadrach, Meshach, and Abed-Nego, and cast them into the burning fiery furnace. Then these men were bound in their coats, their trousers, their turbans, and their other garments, and were cast into the midst of the burning fiery furnace. Therefore, because the king's command was urgent, and the furnace exceedingly hot, the flame of the fire killed those men who took up Shadrach, Meshach, and Abed-Nego. And these three men, Shadrach, Meshach, and Abed-Nego, fell down bound into the midst of the burning fiery furnace.

Then King Nebuchadnezzar was astonished; and he rose in haste and spoke, saying to his counselors, "Did we not cast three men bound into the midst of the fire?" They answered and said to the king, "True, O king." "Look!" he answered, "I see four men loose, walking in the midst of the fire; and they are not hurt, and the form of the fourth is like the Son of God."

Daniel 3:8-25

The three young Jewish men who are the focus of this amazing story are actually slaves. King Nebuchadnezzar conquered Judah and took many of the children of Israel as captive in Babylon. These weren't just "ordinary, run-of-the-mill" slaves. These were highly educated, gifted, wise and knowledgeable young people who had abilities that would serve the king in various capacities of leadership. Each of these young men possessed extraordinary abilities and the King appointed them over the affairs of the provinces of Babylon. Everything was going great until the king had an idea to not only set up a false idol of gold, but to demand that every single person in Babylon bow down and worship it.

That wasn't going to happen with Shadrach, Meschach and Abednego! These three young, Hebrew men were committed to the Lord God Jehovah and refused to bow down to a false god, no matter how big it was or who set it up.

Scholars suggest that this enormous image was most likely an image of Nebuchadnezzer, himself. If that is the case, he was demanding that his subjects recognize him as the embodiment of divine power and required them to worship him in recognition of his personal strength. As Hebrews, these young men were taught not to worship false idols and to do so would put them in a place of betrayal to the one true God. Needless to say, this enraged the Babylonians and particularly Nebuchadnezzer. Upon their insistence that they would not bow down to a false idol, the decree was issued that they would be thrown into a fiery furnace. The king was so angry that he ordered the furnace to be heated seven times hotter than normal.

Upon hearing the dictate that they would be executed, the response of the three Hebrew young men was that under no conditions would they worship a false god and if they were thrown into the furnace, God would rescue them and even if He didn't they still weren't going to bow!

God supernaturally met these young warriors at the very point of their need. Not only did the Lord protect them from the flames, but joined the party! When the king looked into the furnace, he saw that not only did the young men survive, but that there was a fourth person in there, and he recognized him as the Son of God.

Shadrach, Meshach and Abednego were brought out of the furnace, and the heart of the king was turned to the Lord. In spite of the cultural pressures, the expectations of higher authorities and the threat of death, we find young men who reach deeper into their hearts and make a decision to stand on their values and virtues and leave the outcome to the Lord. Their trust and confidence was not betrayed and they were delivered, and ultimately, promoted!

Lessons of Victory

Even if we Burn, we will not Turn. These Hebrew young men had a lot to lose. Even though they were slaves, they had been promoted to some pretty lofty positions and were considered extremely important. It would have been easy for them to justify bowing down to an idol. After all, they were in a foreign land and "when in Rome, do as the Romans". They could easily have said that they were "just going through the motions" and really didn't mean it in their heart. However, their heart of commitment dictated their external actions and they refused to turn against the Lord their God. One of the most astounding dynamics of this story is their statement of conviction that God would most certainly deliver them from the furnace, but even if He didn't, they still would not bow. Being eternally anchored in your soul will set the standard of how you live your life. None of these young men were willing to compromise their beliefs even if it meant death. Our Christianity is not about going to church on Sundays and then living like the rest of the world throughout the week. God is not looking for people who are "convenient Christians", He is looking for those that are willing to lay down their lives for the sake of the gospel. Comfortable Christians will not "go into all the world" unless there is something in it for them. They will not take up their cross daily, unless there is a pay-off at the end of the day. Taking up your cross means that life is no longer about you. Your passion is to please the Father no matter what the cost. Being willing to burn is about giving up your rights, your fame, your reputation and surrendering to the Lordship of Jesus Christ, no matter what it demands of you, how much you will have to pay or how far you may have to go in order to fulfill the will of God for your life.

I will be with You, even through the Flames. We have a promise from the Lord that He "will never leave us or forsake us" (Hebrews 13:5). God is for you and not against you. He sees when you are walking through the good times and He knows when you are walking through the fire. He is committed to your success in life and surrounds you on every side with His grace, love and mercy. Isaiah 43:2 says "When you pass through the waters, I *will be* with you; And through the rivers, they shall not overflow you. When you walk through the fire, you shall not be burned, Nor shall the flame scorch you." God never promises that we will not pass through the waters or that we will not walk through the fire. What He does promise is that when we do walk through the waters of life and the fiery trials that come, He will be with us. There is a confused teaching that circulates in the Body of Christ that God brings calamity into your life to teach you certain things. Nothing could be further from the truth! God does not bring calamity upon His children. He protects us through the trials and tribulations and uses them to shape and fashion us into His image. The lessons of life can come from anywhere, but what we know of God is that He doesn't waste anything that we go through. He is more concerned about the outcome of your character than the resolve of the situation you may find yourself in. Submitting to the Lord no matter what you are facing in life will bring you to a place of impartation, supernatural investment and being molded into the person that He has ordained you to be.

Protection and Promotion. As we have already seen, God's will is to protect His children no matter what they are facing in life. However, I don't want us to miss the fact that the posture that these young men took opened up the door for the promotion of God in their lives. The very last verse of Daniel chapter three simply says that "the king promoted Shadrach, Meshach and Abednego, in the province of Babylon" (Daniel 3:30). The word promoted is the Hebrew word "tsalach" and it means "to cause to prosper, to show prosperity and to be successful". Success is never an accident. People who become "successful" in life by happenstance, normally do not stay that way very long. Doing what is right in the moment is the very thing that will set you up for success in the future. It is normally not the big things and the big decisions that bring success into your life, but being faithful, steadfast, consistent and honorable in the daily decisions of your life. These young men were able to be faithful in a major moment of decision because they had been taught to be faithful to God as they lived their lives. Bowing down to an idol was not an issue. They had already settled the issues in their hearts and the integrity required was something that was not foreign to them. It is not in the heat of the battle when you must make a decision in terms of who you are and how you will respond. Your character is shaped and fashioned in the daily grind of life and the little decisions that you must make. Your integrity is determined by the responses that are a part of who you are, what you value and how you esteem others. Building up and strengthening your character will always pay off when the big moment arrives and that is what makes you a candidate for the promotions that come from the Lord.

TODAY'S CONFESSION OF VICTORY

The size of the idol is not the issue. The one who erected the idol is not the issue. The issue is whether or not I will bow to the spirit of compromise and sacrifice my integrity at the altar of convenience, self-promotion or protection. I stake my claim today! I am a born-again, child of God, called by His name and I will not bend, I will not bow, I will not break. I stand steadfast in the face of the demonic. I rise up in faith against the lies of hell that would attempt to tower over my life and demand my loyalty or set themselves up as worthy of my attention. Jesus is Lord over my life and my family. I serve Him and Him alone. I will not warm myself to strange fires, I will not listen to or entertain the voice of a stranger. I walk in integrity and I trust God, His plans, purposes and promotion to come to fruition in who I am and in who I am becoming.

Day Twenty Three

IN THE LION'S DEN

"So the king gave the order, and they brought Daniel and threw him into the lions' den. The king said to Daniel, "May your God, whom you serve continually, rescue you!" A stone was brought and placed over the mouth of the den, and the king sealed it with his own signet ring and with the rings of his nobles, so that Daniel's situation might not be changed. Then the king returned to his palace and spent the night without eating and without any entertainment being brought to him. And he could not sleep.

At the first light of dawn, the king got up and hurried to the lions' den. When he came near the den, he called to Daniel in an anguished voice, "Daniel, servant of the living God, has your God, whom you serve continually, been able to rescue you from the lions?" Daniel answered, "May the king live forever! My God sent his angel, and he shut the mouths of the lions. They have not hurt me, because I was found innocent in his sight. Nor have I ever done any wrong before you, Your Majesty."

The king was overjoyed and gave orders to lift Daniel out of the den. And when Daniel was lifted from the den, no wound was found on him, because he had trusted in his God."

Daniel 6:16-23

Daniel is still a captive in Babylon. God has given him favor and he has been promoted as the third highest authority, with the king planning on establishing him over the entire kingdom. While that is a blessing for Daniel, not everybody in the kingdom is happy. Daniel established himself over all the governors and rulers because of the spirit of excellence that he operated in and many were jealous of him. Out of their jealousy, they schemed against him to establish a law that those who worshipped anybody but the king for a period of thirty days would be cast into a den of lions, knowing that Daniel would continue his faithfulness towards Yahweh in spite of their foolish laws.

When Daniel learned of the decree, he went home and continued his faithful practice of worship and prayer unto the Lord. The evil administrators had him right where they wanted him. Because the law could not be reversed, at sundown he was thrown into the den of lions, hoping that he would never be seen again. But God! What the administrators did not take into consideration was that the very God to whom Daniel prayed, was the same God who created the lions and was able to shut their mouths against Daniel, and that's exactly what He did.

Early the next morning, the king ran to the lion's den and found that Daniel was safe and sound. God had spared him because of his innocence and faithfulness. The king promptly recognized that Daniel had been set up and had the very men who conspired against him thrown into the lion's den where they immediately lost their lives. In response to Daniel's faith, the king issued another decree that the people were to reverence and fear the God of Daniel.

Lessons of Victory

The easy way out is not always the Best way out. Daniel refused to abandon his faith in God and take the easy way out. Even though he was faced with the potential of an agonizing death, he did not falter in his confidence in God as his deliverer. Daniel's name means "God is my Judge", and in his conviction of God's ability to see the integrity of his heart, he trusted in the Lord to see his innocence and protect him, no matter what came against him.

For Daniel to have taken the "easy way out" means that he would have to compromise his integrity as well as his faith. In his response, it becomes apparent that Daniel is a man who is living for eternity and carries a deep conviction that to compromise his faith would be a greater sin than to adhere to the folly of men. The demand placed upon him pales in comparison to the depth of passion, fervor and fire that he carries in his heart for the Lord.

The path of integrity is often filled with challenges and plenty of opportunities to deny yourself of the pleasures and comforts of life. The road to compromise may seem shorter, and not as difficult to navigate, but is actually takes you places that you never intended to journey. While the compromise seems promising, it will normally end up costing you more and demanding more of you than you ever intended to give.

Daniel was not ashamed of His God. Faced with the consequences of a heart that would not compromise, Daniel knew that his next prayer could very well be his last. It would have certainly been easy for him to hide himself in his prayer closet, to become a private citizen of Yahweh's kingdom or to justify that because he was being plotted against, he would just lay low until the scrutiny subsided. Actually, boldness rose up in Daniel's heart and he threw open the window, turned to Jerusalem and began to have a worship service, just as he always did! Not only did Daniel pray once but, as was his custom, he prayed three times a day. Daniel had a reputation in the king's palace and administration, but he also had a reputation for being a committed follower of God.

The temptation for so many is to be one person at work and

somebody else when they are at church. God is calling you to throw upon the window and have a testimony of being a believer, no matter where you are, what circumstances you find yourself in or who are might be around. Paul said that he "was not ashamed of the gospel of Christ, for it is the power of God unto salvation" (Romans 1:16). The word ashamed in this scripture means to dishonor. Paul is saying that he refuses to dishonor the sacrifices that Jesus made for his salvation by being embarrassed to admit that he is a Christian. It is through your life that others will find the goodness and the power of God that is available for them. Don't send mixed messages. Be a man or woman after the heart of God, twenty-four hours a day, seven days a week.

Confidence in the Midst of A Crisis. This was not the first challenge that Daniel faced in his life and it wouldn't be the last. Whenever you are faced with a conflict that is contrary to the will and purposes of God and you choose God's will instead of following after your own desires, you strengthen and deepen your commitment to Him. In times like this, when your faith is challenged and tested, your Christian character is being shaped and fashioned, and if you stand steadfast, you come out of the trial even stronger than before.

TODAY'S CONFESSION OF VICTORY

I will stand in faith and confidence and declare the Lordship of Jesus over my life, no matter what the challenge. I place my complete trust and confidence in the Lord and know that in my boldness, I will be vindicated. I do not fear what man can do to me. I trust in the power of God to shut the mouths of the lions as well as the mouths of evildoers who rise up against who I am and what I believe. I open the window of my life for all to see that I stand in confidence of what God has done in my life and I will never be ashamed of the gospel of Jesus Christ.

I carry a fervor and a fire for Jesus in my heart and I will shout it from the rooftops so that all will hear, all will see and all will know that I am the redeemed of God!

Day Twenty Four

FOR SUCH A TIME AS THIS

"The king loved Esther more than all the other women, and she obtained grace and favor in his sight more than all the virgins; so he set the royal crown upon her head and made her queen instead of Vashti. Then the king made a great feast, the Feast of Esther, for all his officials and servants; and he proclaimed a holiday in the provinces and gave gifts according to the generosity of a king.

And all the king's servants who were within the king's gate bowed and paid homage to Haman, for so the king had commanded concerning him. But Mordecai would not bow or pay homage. Then the king's servants who were within the king's gate said to Mordecai, "Why do you transgress the king's command?" Now it happened, when they spoke to him daily and he would not listen to them, that they told it to Haman, to see whether Mordecai's words would stand; for Mordecai had told them that he was a Jew. When Haman saw that Mordecai did not bow or pay him homage, Haman was filled with wrath. Then Haman said to King Ahasuerus, "There is a certain people scattered and dispersed among the people in all the provinces of your kingdom; their laws are different from all other people's, and they do not keep the king's laws. Therefore it is not fitting for the king to let them remain. If it pleases the king, let a decree be written that they be destroyed, and I will pay ten thousand talents of silver into the hands of those who do the work, to bring it into the king's treasuries." So the king took his signet ring from his hand and gave it to Haman, the son of Hammedatha the Agagite, the enemy of the Jews. And the king said to Haman, "The money and the people are given to you, to do with them as seems good to you." When Mordecai learned all that had happened, he tore his clothes and put on sackcloth and ashes, and went out into the midst of the city. He cried out with a loud and bitter cry. He went as far as the front of the king's gate, for no one might enter the king's gate clothed with sackcloth.

And in every province where the king's command and decree arrived, there was great mourning among the Jews, with fasting, weeping, and wailing; and many lay in sackcloth and ashes."

And Mordecai told them to answer Esther: "Do not think in your heart that you will escape in the king's palace any more than all the other Jews. For if you remain completely silent at this time, relief and deliverance will arise for the Jews from another place, but you and your father's house will perish. Yet who knows whether you have come to the kingdom for such a time as this?"

Then Esther told them to reply to Mordecai: "Go, gather all the Jews who are present in Shushan, and fast for me; neither eat nor drink for three days, night or day. My maids and I will fast likewise. And so I will go to the king, which is against the law; and if I perish, I perish!" So Mordecai went his way and did according to all that Esther commanded him.

Now it happened on the third day that Esther put on her royal robes and stood in the inner court of the king's palace, across from the king's house, while the king sat on his royal throne in the royal house, facing the entrance of the house. So it was, when the king saw Queen Esther standing in the court, that she found favor in his sight, and the king held out to Esther the golden scepter that was in his hand. Then Esther went near and touched the top of the scepter.

And the king said to her, "What do you wish, Queen Esther? What is your request? It shall be given to you—up to half the kingdom!" So Esther answered, "If it pleases the king, let the king and Haman come today to the banquet that I have prepared for him."

Then Queen Esther answered and said, "If I have found favor in your sight, O king, and if it pleases the king, let my life be given me at my petition, and my people at my request. For we have been sold, my people and I, to be destroyed, to be killed, and to be annihilated. Had we been sold as male and female slaves, I would have held my tongue, although the enemy could never compensate for the king's loss."

So King Ahasuerus answered and said to Queen Esther, "Who is he, and where is he, who would dare presume in his heart to do such a thing?" And Esther said, "The adversary and enemy is this wicked Haman!"

Esther 2:17-18, 3:2-5, 8-10, 4:1-3, 15-17, 7:3-6

There is a lot going on in this story! It begins with the king who is having marital problems. King Ahasuerus wanted to spend some time with his wife, but she refused. Her refusal didn't actually turn out good for her. She discovered pretty quickly that kings aren't used to being told no. The king decides to replace her and now he's on the search for a new queen. He decides to hold somewhat of a competition and have all of the virgins of the land appear before him.

When a young girl named Hadassah appears before the king, the competition is over! He finds himself smitten by her beauty, charm and grace. His favor was extended to this young maiden, her name was changed to Esther and she became the queen. Everything was good in the kingdom, except for the fact that this beautiful young queen held a secret that even the king was not aware of. She was Jewish.

Esther had an uncle named Mordecai, who unwittingly found himself in the middle of the royal drama, by the fact that he had actually saved the king's life from assassins. His intervention gained him favor with the king, but pitted him against an evil man named Haman, who wanted to annihilate all of the Jews. Through an evil and manipulative scheme, Haman deceived the king into signing an order that would execute the Jewish people, for nothing more than being Jewish. When Mordecai heard about the plot, he was devastated and invoked the favor of his niece, the queen. He was convinced that she had "come into the kingdom for such a time as this".

Throughout this life-threatening ordeal, the true and pure heart of Esther was revealed. Without hesitation, she agreed to approach the king, even if it cost her life. With no invitation, she went into the king's presence and the favor of God prevailed. He was delighted to see her, honored and favored her and heard her request. Because of her intervention on behalf of her people, Haman was exposed and ultimately put to death and the lives of the Jewish people were spared.

Lessons of Victory

God always has bigger plans. Hadassah was a beautiful young woman and won the heart of the king. One would think that becoming the queen or being elevated to a lofty position or place in life would be the epitome of life, but God had even bigger plans for her. Your promotions in life always hold a greater purpose than just your personal provision. Like Esther, you "were born for such a time as this". The divine purposes of God include your promotion but like God told Abraham, "I am blessing you, so that you can be a blessing to the nations." We all have a choice to make, and when our lives are poured out for others, God has no problem blessing you because you become a conduit of His life and love to others as opposed to gathering all of His blessings unto yourself.

The "Kairos" moments of God are Divinely orchestrated to fulfill His purposes through you. Most of us live our lives with a "chronos" mentality. Chronos is measured by clocks, calendars, schedules and a multitude of appointments. The Greek word "kairos" means the opportune moments. Chronos requires discipline and punctuality. Kairos requires discipline and discernment or spiritual sensitivity. In actuality, we need both. A healthy balance in life allows for a chronos structure, in which the kairos moments can be fulfilled. Life is not about sitting around waiting for the perfect moment, but listening with a sensitive and obedient ear and having a willingness to respond with a heart that pursues the passions of God at any moment.

In a chronos world, it was quite inconvenient for Esther to approach the king, but because she took advantage of the moment, she found favor, blessing and ultimately life, not only for herself, but for her people.

Freedom and Deliverance are the Result of a life before the Lord. It's interesting, because in the book of Esther; God, Himself is never mentioned. Notwithstanding, it is apparent that they were seeking a heavenly response from Jehovah based on their fasting, weeping and intercession. God heard their cry and had actually already responded through the life of a young, beautiful woman who found herself in a place that she never could have imagined possible. A mentor of mine always says that the "degree of authority that you have *in* God is directly related to the degree of intimacy that you have *with* God". We are constantly in the need of grace and divine intervention. The very thing that gives birth to His grace and mercy is our personal relationship with Him, our prayer and fasting. Your life before the Lord opens the portals of heaven, removes demonic distractions, exposes demonic intentions, and releases the abundance of God's provisions.

God will use everything and everybody for His divine Purpose. Our lives are not up for grabs and nothing goes to waste. God is absolutely in control of every aspect of who we are and the world in which we live. Heaven and earth are subject to His authority, purposes and plans. In this story, God intersected several lives and circumstances so that His will would ultimately be realized. Even when you can't recognize God's hand in various situations, as a believer, you can have confidence in knowing that God is always redemptive and that He always uses every single thing to work out His will on your behalf.

TODAY'S CONFESSION OF VICTORY

God's plans for my life exceed my lack of vision or the circumstances in which I find myself. God has a promotion planned for me that will be used to be a blessing to those in my world. I am an open vessel and a conduit for His blessings to pour through. I am sensitive to the leading and moving of the Holy Spirit and am ready to respond in obedience to the opportunities that He sets before me. I walk by faith and not by sight!

Day Twenty Five

GET BEHIND ME

"Then Jesus, being filled with the Holy Spirit, returned from the Jordan and was led by the Spirit into the wilderness, being tempted for forty days by the devil. And in those days He ate nothing, and afterward, when they had ended, He was hungry. And the devil said to Him, "If You are the Son of God, command this stone to become bread."

But Jesus answered him, saying, "It is written, 'Man shall not live by bread alone, but by every word of God.' " Then the devil, taking Him up on a high mountain, showed Him all the kingdoms of the world in a moment of time. And the devil said to Him, "All this authority I will give You, and their glory; for this has been delivered to me, and I give it to whomever I wish. Therefore, if You will worship before me, all will be Yours."

And Jesus answered and said to him, "Get behind Me, Satan! For it is written, 'You shall worship the LORD your God, and Him only you shall serve.' " Then he brought Him to Jerusalem, set Him on the pinnacle of the temple, and said to Him, "If You are the Son of God, throw Yourself down from here. For it is written: 'He shall give His angels charge over you,

To keep you,' and, 'In their hands they shall bear you up, Lest you dash your foot against a stone.' "

And Jesus answered and said to him, "It has been said, 'You shall not tempt the LORD your God.' " Now when the devil had ended every temptation, he departed from Him until an opportune time."

Luke 4:1-13

Jesus has just come out of an amazing time of revival. He has been freshly filled with the Holy Spirit, baptized by the wilderness prophet John and received and awesome word of confirmation from the Lord. Following that, He received specific instruction from the Lord to go out into the wilderness on a getaway camping trip to spend time fasting and praying. Along comes the devil. Nobody knows how to ruin a good time and rain on your revival like the devil!

Much like he did with Adam and Even in the Garden of Eden, he approached Jesus with deceptive words, demonic intentions and promises of grandeur. This was the big moment. Would Jesus stand steadfast and resist him, thus securing his immanent defeat or would He cave in to the lies and give the enemy exactly what he was looking for? Had Jesus done any of the things that he was tempted to, He would have had to exercise His authority as God and that would have forfeited His right to go to the cross as the Son of Man. Although Jesus was fully God, He never exercised any level of authority as God. He came to the earth as a man and he would have to die as a man in order to fulfill the sacrificial requirement to redeem man. It was a natural earth-born man that lost the original covenant and it would have to be a natural earth-born man that regained the right to that covenant.

The devil came at Jesus from every angle. He tempted him; spirit, soul and body. Jesus was having none of it. He resisted the enemy by virtue of the Word of God. He stood on what He knew and who He was. He did not engage the devil in His own strength, but the strength of the Word. It's interesting because every single thing that satan offered to Jesus would ultimately become His anyway.

Lessons of Victory

<u>Some of Life's Greatest Lessons are Learned in the Wilderness.</u>
The term "wilderness" means different things to different people.
The literal definition is "an uncultivated, uninhabited, and
inhospitable region. In a spiritual sense, the word refers to a place
where there is no good or truth, and where good is not conjoined
with truth. There were three specific places that Jesus was
required to reach deep within Himself in order to accomplish the
purposes of God for Him on the earth: the wilderness, the garden
and on Golgotha. In each of those situations, it was mandated
upon Jesus that He walk in complete obedience and fulfill the
purposes of God in that moment.

It's not always in the good times that God will show Himself to
you. Sometimes it's when things aren't so good. Sometimes it's
when the odds are stacked against you and you aren't quite
certain who you are, where to go or what to do. While the
wilderness can be harsh, it's also very enlightening and enabling,
in terms of gaining a perspective that eludes you when you aren't
necessarily desperate. Don't be afraid of the wilderness times or
seasons in your life. Welcome them, embrace them, knowing that
the Father surrounds you with His great love and that His all-
consuming passion for you will protect you even in the harshest
of wilderness experiences. Open your mind and your heart to the
lessons of the wilderness. Breathe in the air of discomfort and
allow it to penetrate the hardened chambers of your heart and
bring you to a new place of understanding, strength and
confirmation that comes only from the wilderness.

<u>God will never Tempt you, but He will Test You.</u> God
intentionally led Jesus into the wilderness knowing that He was

going to encounter the enemy. God was not tempting Jesus, but He was testing Him. Temptation carries an unmistakable sense of the demonic that is designed to discourage, distract and defeat you. Every element of temptation is crafted in the bowels of hell and the sole purpose of it is to disconnect you from your anointing. God is incapable of tempting you.

What was happening in this wilderness experience was a testing that would serve to propel Jesus into a new level of life and authority. In fact, when you continue to read this story, you find that it was actually the prelude to the launching of the ministry of Jesus. "Then Jesus returned in the power of the Spirit to Galilee, and news of Him went out through all the surrounding region. And He taught in their synagogues, being glorified by all" (Luke 4:14-15). The testing of the Father ultimately brings promotion and power into your life. On the other hand, temptation is designed to be destructive in your life. It's been said that the test will become a testimony!

The Wilderness Reveals who you Are. Jesus was who He was, far before He went into the wilderness. He didn't become faithful to the heart of the Father and the standard of the Word of God in the wilderness, He was already faithful, strong and committed. The wilderness was nothing more than the proving ground for who He already was. It's in the wilderness that your character is revealed. It's in the wilderness that the inner strength that you have been building is called upon and brought to the surface. You can't wait until you get to the wilderness to decide who you are.

Your daily investment into your spiritual growth shows up when conditions are harsh, supplies are limited, encouragement is sparse and the enemy is breathing down your neck. Don't wait. If you go into the wilderness hungry, lacking and spiritually dry, you will be vulnerable and easy prey for the enemy. Decide now who you are, what you are about and who you belong to!

<u>Your diet must include the Bread of Heaven.</u> The enemy came to Jesus when He was hungry. He had been fasting for forty days and was at a place of physical destitution. Under those conditions, Jesus was in a place where it would have been easy to give in to extreme conditions and satisfy his physical hunger. The word that was used for bread is the Greek word "artos" and it carried the connotation of more than just a simple loaf of bread, but specifically referred to the bread used at the table of the Lord for Passover. Ultimately, it became the bread of communion. The enemy wasn't looking for Jesus just to satisfy His natural hunger, but was inviting Him to a demonic table of communion. "Come, allow me to satisfy your carnal cravings and natural desires", "Commune with me and fellowship with darkness." The invitations of the enemy always have greater consequences than just a natural fulfillment but venture into the spiritual. Communion is agreement and that was the ultimate goal of the enemy. Had Jesus come into agreement with him, it would have solidified the enemy's rule and reign over mankind and over the earth. Jesus was a man on a mission, He had already been eating from the bread of heaven and was not swayed by the invitation of compromise and collusion with the powers of darkness.

TODAY'S CONFESSION OF VICTORY

Even when I am in the wilderness, You never leave me or forsake me. I have a promise of Your presence and I rest in the grace of who You are in me. I stand confident in who I am in You and I will not be moved by what I see, think, hear or feel. My test is becoming my testimony and God is using the difficulties to strengthen me, build me up and promote me. I have a deep desire to know the Father and my heart is continually being shaped and fashioned by His love that washes over me. When I am in the wilderness, I still find clarity because of who God is in me. The wilderness doesn't break me, but brings my anointing and the favor of God to the surface of my life. My mind, my heart and my will are in complete agreement with the purposes of God over me, no matter what season I am in.

Day Twenty Six

UNTO US

"Now the birth of Jesus Christ was as follows: after His mother Mary was betrothed to Joseph, before they came together, she was found with child of the Holy Spirit. Then Joseph her husband, being a just man, and not wanting to make her a public example, was minded to put her away secretly. But while he thought about these things, behold, an angel of the Lord appeared to him in a dream, saying, "Joseph, son of David, do not be afraid to take to you Mary your wife, for that which is conceived in her is of the Holy Spirit. And she will bring forth a Son, and you shall call His name JESUS, for He will save His people from their sins."

So all this was done that it might be fulfilled which was spoken by the Lord through the prophet, saying: "Behold, the virgin shall be with child, and bear a Son, and they shall call His name Immanuel," which is translated, "God with us."

Then Joseph, being aroused from sleep, did as the angel of the Lord commanded him and took to him his wife, and did not know her till she had brought forth her firstborn Son. And he called His name JESUS."

Matthew 1:18-25

Without a doubt, this is THE greatest story of victory in the Bible! The world is about to change forever. Plunged into darkness by an insidious and evil plot staged by the master deceiver in the Garden of Eden, the world has been waiting for this moment. True to heavenly form, in that He uses the foolish things of the world to confound the wise; God chooses a simple, Jewish girl that possesses a pure heart to overthrow a demonic hierarchy that has been in rule for centuries. Most Christian theologians agree that Mary was most likely between fifteen to sixteen years of age at the time of the birth of Christ. She hardly would have been a likely candidate to bring about world change that would affect all of history as it was known and altar eternity, but that's exactly what happened!

Just imagine, what could not be accomplished by tribes of priests, prophets, rabbis and holy men, systems of sacrifices, commandments and years of attempting to keep strict levitical laws, was achieved by a young teenage girl who just happened to believe God and was obedient to His word. To get her attention, God staged a pretty dramatic encounter with an archangel as well as appearing to her fiancé, Joseph in a dream. Both of these young people responded to this heavenly intervention with a heart that was desirous of God's perfect will in their lives and a submission to an extraordinary vision that would literally bring the kingdom of God back to the earth realm.

Mary submitted herself to the will of God and brought forth a child, born of a virgin. He was the Messiah and she called His name Jesus. He is Immanuel, God with us. This amazing story reflects not only the willing and gracious heart of a young virgin and her confused fiancé, but reveals the depth and the passion of our Father God, who in the form of Jesus, left His heavenly realm, submitted Himself to the limitations of earth beings and eventually became the sacrificial lamb of God, thus answering the sin issue for all of eternity.

Lessons of Victory

It all comes down to Choices. Like all of us, Mary had a choice. In fact, she had several choices. She could have easily responded in fear, but she chose faith. She could have been disobedient, but she chose to obey. Mary could have simply chosen not to participate in what seemed like an unlikely possibility, but she responded with a heart of submission, "be it unto me, according to your word..." (Luke 1:38). Without a doubt, Mary had to have considered the rumors, gossip and innuendos that would plaque her for the rest of her life. Not only do virgins not have babies, but this certainly is NOT how the Messiah is going to appear according to Jewish understanding.

None of that moved Mary because she chose to follow what she knew was the heart and the will of God for her life and for the world. She set herself in agreement with God and the consequences that would follow would be His responsibility, not hers. Even if others did mock her, she was willing to endure the mockery in order to fulfill the will of God. In all of our lives, it comes down to choices. You are who you are today because of the choices that you made yesterday. While none of us can change the past, we are required to live with the consequences of the choices that we have made in the past, both good and bad. It's been said, "one word from God can change your life forever" so can one choice. Choices are life changing. May we be reminded of the power of choice as we observe the obedience of Mary and how that one choice changed each of our lives.

The Power of Agreement. I'm sure that Mary could have managed the birth of Jesus by herself as a single mother, but God had other plans. He wanted Jesus to have an earthly father who would surround him with the grace and nurturing that a father brings. This couldn't be just any man, it had to be a man that had the ability to hear the voice of the Lord, follow Him in obedience and support His wife and a child that wasn't his own flesh and blood. This divine assignment required the power of agreement. I believe that the greatest power on earth is the power of love and the second greatest power is agreement. "Again I say unto you, that if two of you shall agree on earth concerning anything that they shall ask, it shall be done for them by My Father who is in Heaven" (Matthew 18:19). Agreement literally activates the hand of God and releases the provision of God in your life.

Find people of faith who will stand with you, no matter what it looks like in the natural and when others may not understand. Connect with those who will be willing to go the extra mile with you and stand with you even when the circumstances seem contradictory. Be careful to align yourself with people of like precious faith and those that walk in integrity and will protect you. Refuse to come into agreement with those that are walking in fear, doubt or unbelief. Your breakthrough could very well depend on proper alignment with those that are walking in faith and conviction and under the authority of the word of God.

Jesus was fully God and fully Man. His name shall be called Immanuel, which means "God with Us." This is a very important theological scripture that establishes two very important doctrines. Firstly, God came to earth in the form of Jesus as the heavenly sacrifice for the sins of mankind and secondly, that Jesus absolutely was God. Whenever you hear the name Immanuel, the incarnation becomes deeply personal. The longing of God to be with us reveals the heart of passion and love that He has for us. To utter the name of Immanuel is to declare hope and life. God is with us to redeem us back to the plans and purposes of the Father. God is with us to heal us and to protect us from the demonic ploys and snares of the enemy. He is with us to redemptively establish His grace and mercy in all that concerns us. The bible declares that He is "our refuge and strength, an ever-present help in the time of need" (Psalm 46:1). He will never leave you nor forsake you

(Hebrews 13:5), because He is Immanuel.

TODAY'S CONFESSION OF VICTORY

Lord, today, like Mary, it is my good confession "be it unto me, according to Your word." You have visited me in my weaknesses and sin and came to me offering love, forgiveness and salvation. Because of Your grace, I can declare that I am the redeemed of God. I walk in grace, mercy and the covering of the word over me and my family. Today, I choose You. I thank You, Lord that You give me wisdom and a heart to follow hard after You, no matter what others may think. I am willing to be, to say or to do anything that is Your will for my life, regardless of how misunderstood I might be. I live for an audience of one and will not expend my energies trying to please man. I stand in agreement with the word and I surround myself with those of like precious faith. I am used of the Lord to encourage others who are also standing on the word. I thank You that You are always with me and that Your rod and staff comfort me and that You will never leave me or forsake me. I am growing in the grace of redemption and I am being shaped and fashioned by the presence of the Lord in my life; spirit, soul and body.

Day Twenty Seven

A NIGHT ON THE SEA

"On the same day, when evening had come, He said to them, "Let us cross over to the other side." *Now when they had left the multitude, they took Him along in the boat as He was. And other little boats were also with Him. And a great windstorm arose, and the waves beat into the boat, so that it was already filling. But He was in the stern, asleep on a pillow. And they awoke Him and said to Him, "Teacher, do You not care that we are perishing?"*

Then He arose and rebuked the wind, and said to the sea, "Peace, be still!" *And the wind ceased and there was a great calm. But He said to them,* "Why are you so fearful? How is it that you have no faith?" *And they feared exceedingly, and said to one another, "Who can this be, that even the wind and the sea obey Him!"*

Mark 4:35-41

In order to fully understand the events that are taking place in this "drama on the water," it is imperative that it be taken into full context. Reading the next chapter, we discover that Jesus is actually on a very specific mission to an area called the Gadarenes. It was there that Jesus confronted the demoniac in the tombs and cast out a legion of devils. That divine encounter brought about a revival in a ten-city area that had been held in darkness, bondage and captivity.

The Sea of Galilee was particularly known for having sudden, violent storms that could occur without notice. With hills on every side of this body of water, the air surrounding the mountains is cooler and the air around the lake would be considered semi-tropical with moist, warm air. When those two varying temperatures collide, the result is the type of storm that the disciples encountered that night. But, that's not what happened here. A closer look will reveal a more sinister plot that was designed in hell for the purposes of circumventing the mission of Jesus and His disciples in the Gadarenes area.

Darkness was falling over the Galilee area with Jesus and His disciples just finishing up a very successful revival meeting with multitudes gathered to hear Him teach the word. Following the meeting, Jesus gave very specific instructions to go to the other side of the lake. In the middle of the lake a great storm arose that had the disciples in fear for their lives. They find Jesus asleep in the boat, causing even further panic among them. Jesus arose, spoke peace to the waves, rebuked the wind and the storm was over.

Lessons of Victory

<u>**Go to the Other Side**</u>. Jesus already had a plan to get the disciples safely to the other side. His directive was not determined by the possibilities of storms, attacks from the enemy or anything that might deter the greater purpose of the trip. Jesus wants to take you to the other side as well! On the other side is a place of deliverance, freedom, ministry and revival.

Crossing the sea is always a place where your fears are challenged and faith is demanded. Somebody asked if God was "safe?" The answer to that question is no, but you can trust Him. That means that there will be times when you are required to attempt things that are not necessarily "safe" in the realm of the natural, but if God calls you to it, you can trust Him. The one thing that you can be confident of is that you are called to the other side. God has not called you to stay in a place of comfort and security, but to launch out into the deep where you are required to trust and rely upon Him.

We're about to Die and You don't Care. Based on the word of the Lord that had already been established, Jesus certainly wasn't concerned about any storm that might arise, and He certainly had no intention for the disciples to perish in that storm. The problem is that the disciples misinterpreted the actions of Jesus. He was completely at peace even in the midst of a major storm, but they saw His ability to sleep as a lack of caring and concern. The lesson for us is that even when the Lord's presence does not seem obvious to us, His abiding word is actually enough. You have a covenant with God that is full of His promises over you. There will be times when you don't "feel" God's presence or that your prayers are being answered. During those times, you stand on the word that has already been given to you. In fact, it's been placed in writing! The Bible is His last will and testament and you can rest assured that His word is His will and His will is His word.

Why are You so Fearful? Jesus countered their concerns with a concern of His own. His concern was relative to their lack of faith and their fear. This clearly illustrates to us that whenever you begin to walk in fear, it is impossible to walk in faith. In fact, you can't walk in faith and fear at the same time, the choice is up to you. The rebuke of Jesus in that moment could only have meant that He expected them to operate in faith. Jesus had already been teaching them principles of faith and how to exercise authority. They had already witnessed His divine power in action on many occasions and actually carried the anointing to deal with this storm issue themselves. The very thing that Jesus did, they were capable of doing also. They had authority over all the elements that were producing the storm. Many times, we are expecting

God to intervene in our lives, when He is expecting us to exercise our faith and authority, stand on the word and deal with the situation. You have been anointed and authorized to be God's ambassador on the earth and dominion has been given to you as a believer!

<u>Jesus spoke peace to the Waves, and Rebuked the Wind.</u> This is actually one of the most important lessons of this story. It's imperative that you not miss the point that Jesus did two separate things: He spoke peace to the waves, but He rebuked the wind. There are two specific Greek words that are used in reference to this storm: "lailaps" and "anemos", the combination and usage of these two words gives us insight into why Jesus rebuked the wind. This was no ordinary wind. It was a tempestuous, violent and agitated storm that originated from the cardinal winds of the demonic, thus the rebuke. Jesus identified that the source of this storm was demonic and He was directly rebuking the spirit that was responsible for it.

The effect that this demonically induced storm was having on the waves, was in fact, the actual cause of concern for the disciples. As the waves grew larger, so did their fear. It was the result of the storm that Jesus spoke peace to. Many times as believers, we are tempted to rebuke the circumstances or sometimes even people, when the real issue at hand is the manipulative and tormenting winds of the demonic. God would have us declare peace over the circumstances and those that are involved. Our battle is never with flesh and blood, but principalities, powers and workers of iniquity (Ephesians 6:12).

TODAY'S CONFESSION OF VICTORY

I am going to the other side! I have been called of God to minister deliverance, salvation and freedom and I will not be deterred, no matter what storms may arise. I will not be afraid of the journey. I launch out into the deep knowing that God is always with me and that He has already secured my future and my destiny. I trust His word over me and I will not be moved by the reports and lies that are contrary with His revealed word over my life. I know that my Father loves me, cares for me and surrounds me with His grace, mercy and protection. Even when I cannot emotionally feel His presence, I walk by faith and not by sight. I declare peace to the people that are in my life. Even when those that are close to me are agitated and bothered by the circumstances and issues of life, I speak peace over them. I rebuke the winds of the demonic that rise up against me and take my stand of faith against the lies, strategies and manipulations of hell. His word abides in me and the greater One lives on the inside of me. He rules and reigns supreme over my life, regardless of storms, winds, waves or spirits that would attempt to convince me otherwise.

Day Twenty Eight

ARISE, MY FRIEND

"Now a certain man was sick, Lazarus of Bethany, the town of Mary and her sister Martha. It was that Mary who anointed the Lord with fragrant oil and wiped His feet with her hair, whose brother Lazarus was sick. Therefore the sisters sent to Him, saying, "Lord, behold, he whom You love is sick." When Jesus heard that, He said, "This sickness is not unto death, but for the glory of God, that the Son of God may be glorified through it." So when Jesus came, He found that he had already been in the tomb four days.

Now when He had said these things, He cried with a loud voice, "Lazarus, come forth!" *And he who had died came out bound hand and foot with grave clothes, and his face was wrapped with a cloth. Jesus said to them,* "Loose him, and let him go."*

John 11: 1-4, 17, 43-44

Like Mary and Martha, most of us have been in the unfortunate place where we have had to deal with the death of a loved one. The Bible describes death as "the last great enemy" (1 Corinthians 15:26). While the death of a loved one is certainly one of the most difficult times we will ever walk through, all of us will ultimately face our own death according to Hebrews 9:27, "it is appointed unto men once to die." In this story, these two sisters are deeply grieving because of the death of their brother, Lazarus. Jesus is on His way to see Lazarus and to be with the sisters, but what they don't know is that Jesus is about to reverse the hold that death has on their brother and bring him back to the land of the living! There are many dynamics to this story that deserve a much closer look, but a couple that absolutely demand our attention. We see that from an earlier conversation, Jesus had every intention of raising His friend from the dead. However, in an interesting turn of events, once He saw His friend lying in a tomb, He began to weep. Even though He was going to raise him up, just the very thought of his death was agonizing for Jesus and in this tender moment, we catch of glimpse of His great love for Lazarus, as well as His humanity.

In an awesome display of both surrender to the will of the Father and relational authority that He had with Him, Jesus approached the tomb of Lazarus and conquered death by virtue of the anointing that was on His life. It's important to remember that He wasn't acting as God, but as a man, anointed by God. For a period of four days, the body of Lazarus lay in the grave and while his spirit was in Abraham's bosom. The voice and the authority of Jesus reached beyond the realms of natural life and called His friend back to life!

Lessons of Victory

God's "delays" always make sense to God. Jesus had a reason for waiting four days before He arrived in Bethany. According to Hebrew tradition, when a person dies their "nephesh" hovers above their body for three days. Nephesh is the Hebrew word for soul. The person was considered dead, but on the fourth day, they were unmistakably dead! This wasn't a matter of Jesus calling the spirit of Lazarus back into his body, this was a genuine raising of the dead. This was exactly the type of Messianic miracle that the rabbis had been teaching would happen.

Often, what we consider to be "delays" are not delays at all, but the perfect sequence of events in the prophetic seasons of God over our lives. When we realize that God knows the beginning

174

from the end and that He is weaving the tapestry of our life with loving kindness and heavenly precision, we can relax no matter what happens in the meantime.

Personal Relationship preceded the Remarkable. When Jesus learns that Lazarus is near death, He speaks of him in very tender terms. In fact, He refers to him as His "philos", which is defined as a "very close friend". In no other instance is anyone referred to as the friend of Jesus. Many people in life are looking for a miracle, but in actuality our objective is a heart that pursues, not the miracle, but the One from whom the miracles flow. In order for the supernatural to become the standard by which we live, we must develop a relationship that is based on our desire to be with God, to be like God and a heart that deeply loves Him simply for who He is, not what He does. The level of authority that you experience in your life as a believer, is predicated upon the level of relationship that you have with the Father.

Life Always flows from Jesus. This story records the interesting interactions between Jesus and the two sisters of Lazarus, Mary and Martha. In their deep grief, they are processing a wide range of emotions. The fact that they are close, personal friends with Jesus brings a level of conflict that most would not have to walk through. They are having to reconcile the fact that they have seen Jesus raise people from the dead, and that He could have spoken a word over Lazarus that would have healed him instantly. None of that happened. What they did know, however, was that Jesus loved them and their brother deeply and that He would minister to them regardless. In the face of these unfolding events, there was an air of uncertainty in terms of what would happen next. They knew that something would happen, they just had no idea what it would be. In John 4:14, Jesus declared "whoever drinks of the water that I will give him shall never thirst; but the water that I will give him will become in him a well of water springing up to eternal life."

We live in a dying and decaying world. All around us, we see the processes of death and observe first-hand the effects of the natural cycle of life which includes death. Jesus defeated death and conquered the grave. He is the one that breathes life, health and wholeness into who we are and who we are becoming. While it is true that each of us will face a physical death, the heart of the Father is that we would live life to the fullest and experience the abundance that only a relationship with Him can bring.

Things aren't always as they Appear. To the natural eye, Lazarus was obviously dead. But Jesus wasn't seeing this in the natural. While it is easy to become consumed with what we see with our human eyes, we must remember that we walk by faith and not by sight. I'm reminded of the story of Elisha and his servant. In 2 Kings 6: 17-20, Elisha asks the Lord to open the eyes of his servant, and when He did, it was revealed to him that they were surrounded by horses and chariots of fire. His servant never saw them in the physical realm and often, it's that way with us. God is moving on your behalf even when you're not aware of it. He is setting up divine appointments that you have not even considered. When we are told to "call those things that be not, as though they were" (Romans 4:17), it's because they actually already "are" but have not yet manifested in the physical realm. Your faith reaches into the arena of the spirit and brings into existence those things that are the will of God for your life.

Just because you can't see it, doesn't mean it doesn't exist and just because you don't yet possess it, doesn't mean that it's not yours.

Stand in faith until you see the manifestation, keep believing until what is not seen is seen and keep fighting until the victory is yours!

TODAY'S CONFESSION OF VICTORY

When I was blind, You made me to see. When I was deaf, You gave me ears to hear. When I was dead, You came to me and gave me life. You are my life and my resurrection. You are my all in all and in You, I live, move and have my being. I am coming out of the grave of doubt, fear, unbelief and the stigma that the enemy tries to put on me because I had resided in the grave of unbelief. I am not only coming up out of the grave of despair and small living, but I tear off the grave clothes that would attempt to bind me and keep me from living the fullness of the life and resurrection that I have in you. I have a hope and future. Your word over me is yes and amen. Your love compels me seek Your heart and to believe for the extraordinary life that is found only in You!

Day Twenty Nine

THE TRIUMPHAL ENTRY

(The Yashanah Revelation)

"Now when they drew near Jerusalem, and came to Bethphage, at the Mount of Olives, then Jesus sent two disciples, saying to them, "Go into the village opposite you, and immediately you will find a donkey tied, and a colt with her. Loose them and bring them to Me. And if anyone says anything to you, you shall say, 'The Lord has need of them,' and immediately he will send them."

All this was done that it might be fulfilled which was spoken by the prophet, saying: "Tell the daughter of Zion, 'Behold, your King is coming to you, Lowly, and sitting on a donkey, A colt, the foal of a donkey.' "

So the disciples went and did as Jesus commanded them. They brought the donkey and the colt, laid their clothes on them, and set Him on them. And a very great multitude spread their clothes on the road; others cut down branches from the trees and spread them on the road. Then the multitudes who went before and those who followed cried out, saying:

"Hosanna to the Son of David!
'Blessed is He who comes in the name of the LORD!'
Hosanna in the highest!"

Matthew 21:1-9

Imagine growing up in Israel. Much like Christians today, who look forward to the return of Jesus Christ, the Israelites held a great anticipation of the coming of the Messiah! All of their lives, they had been taught Zechariah 9:9, "Rejoice greatly, O daughter of Zion! Shout in triumph, O daughter of Jerusalem! Behold, your king is coming to you; He is just and endowed with salvation Humble, and mounted on a donkey, Even on a colt, the foal of a donkey".

The coming of the Messiah...dominated every aspect of life and culture for Israel. It was the central focus of the feasts and every man, woman, boy and girl knew all of the signs of the coming Messiah. They cried out to Him in their prayers, come now! They sacrificed in anticipation of His coming! The Coming Messiah was on the heart and on the mind of every Jewish person, all the time! The Israelites were commanded to keep certain feasts throughout the year.

They were commanded to keep seven feasts and one festival, for a total of eight throughout the year. Much like we have certain holidays that we observe and look forward to, Israel was the same. The Feasts were a great time of celebration! The first four feasts were: Passover, Unleavened Bread, First Fruits, Feast of Harvest (Pentecost). The next three Feasts were: Rosh Hashanah (Feast of Trumpets) – New Year, Yom Kippur (Day of Atonement), The Feast of Tabernacles. Our story begins with the Feast of the Tabernacles. The focus of the Feast of Tabernacles was two-fold: The first was to remember God's provision for them when they were in the wilderness. The second was the anticipation and declaration of the coming of the Kingdom of God!

The Israelites would set up small booths or huts on the sides of the homes, their patios, or balconies and would literally move into them for 7 days...it was actually a great party, like camping out. These booths would be decorated with colorful fruit, ribbons, and pictures, and *the tops and sides of them would be made out of palm* _branches._ They were a reminder that the Israelites once lived in flimsy and temporary shelters during their forty years in the wilderness and that they were totally and completely dependent upon the Lord. The Feast Itself: The first and the last days of this 8 day feast, were days of rest...but the seventh day...was known as "Hoshana Rabba" – The Great Day! Hoshana Rabba is a contraction of Hoshiah Na, which means: "The Great Salvation". Put both of those together and you have: "The Great Day of Salvation". Obviously, <u>The Great Day of Salvation is found only in the Messiah!</u> The Great Day was an awesome, wonderful day of national celebration...the worshippers led the way to the Temple where everyone would gather...in great joy and celebration!

The song of the day was Psalm 118: "The voice of rejoicing and salvation is in the tents of the righteous; the right hand of the LORD does valiantly. The right hand of the LORD is exalted; the right hand of the LORD does valiantly. I shall not die, but live, and declare the works of the LORD. I will praise You, for You have answered me, and have become my salvation. Save now, I pray, O LORD; O LORD, I pray, send now prosperity. Blessed is he who comes in the name of the LORD!"

Part of the festivities of the day was the "Water-Drawing Ceremony." The priest had two golden pitchers, one for wine and one for water from the pool of Siloam.

As the wine and the water were poured into the pitchers, the people thanked God for His bounty and for the rain in the coming year. By the way, Jesus stood in the Temple during this great celebration...and declared: "If anyone thirsts, let him come to Me and drink. He who believes in Me, as the Scripture has said, out of his heart will flow rivers of living water" (John 7:37-38). On this seventh day of celebration, the Israelites would gather and march around the temple seven times with their palm branches waving, shouting "Yashanah" which means: <u>save us now, deliver us now, heal us now, prosper us now!</u> At each side of the temple, they would face out, thereby facing the North, South, East and West declaring Yashanah!

They were declaring their thanksgiving for all that God had done, but were also declaring that in the year to come, they would live by virtue of the Yahweh's salvation, deliverance, healing and prosperity. In their proclamation, they were specifically declaring their expectancy of the Messiah, and when He did come, He would come riding into Jerusalem, mounted on a donkey.

Enter Jesus Riding on the Donkey, surrounded by Worshippers! Wait a minute! What's going on here? This is the Feast of the Passover, not the Tabernacle, yet the people were waving their palm branches and shouting, Hosanna! They were celebrating the wrong holiday! It would be like me coming up to you on Easter and saying Merry Christmas!! Hosannah is the English transliteration: It's made up of two words from the Hebrew: Yasha...Save us, and Nah......Now!

Lessons of Victory

<u>**Jesus riding into Jerusalem on the donkey changed everything!**</u>
All of a sudden, everything that they had ever been taught was now being fulfilled before their very eyes! This was prophecy unfolding...this was their prayers being answered! This was the Messiah, and they knew it! They recognized Him, and they cried out to Him: SAVE us Now...Deliver us Now....Heal Us Now...Prosper us Now!!! Yashanah!!

And Jesus (Yeshuah) is our **_Salvation_**, He is our **_Deliverer_**, He is our **_Healer_**, He is our **_Prosperity_**! The Messiah has revealed Himself and we are the recipients of Yashanah!

Today we declare that the Kingdom of God is here! Today, in the same way that Jesus taught His disciples to declare that the kingdom of God would come, so we declare by the shout of Yashanah the kingdom of God to come in our lives, our families, our community, our nation and our world! Israel was taught to declare the coming of the King and His kingdom and then when it came, they missed it. Today, we declare the coming of the Kingdom, but we aren't going to miss it!

"After these things I looked, and behold, a great multitude which no one could number, of all nations, tribes, peoples, and tongues, standing before the throne and before the Lamb, clothed with white robes, with palm branches in their hands, and crying out with a loud voice, saying, "Salvation belongs to our God who sits on the throne, and to the Lamb!" (Revelations 7:9-10).

Make your declaration of Yashanah. Speak over your year, the blessing of the Lord! Declare that the Kingdom of God would come and manifest in your life through salvation, deliverance, healing and prosperity! For Israel, "The Great Day" was once per year at the Feast of Tabernacles. I want to draw your attention to one more verse in the Messianic Psalm 118:24, "This is the day which the Lord has made, I will rejoice and be glad in it." That's everyday for us now, because Jesus is our Yashanah!!

TODAY'S CONFESSION OF VICTORY

Yashanah! Save me now, Heal me now, Deliver me now, Prosper me now! I declare over my life, my family, my community, my nation and my church the blessing of the Lord. The kingdom of God is coming in strength, power and might to save and deliver from the grip of the enemy. My life resounds with God's grace and many shall taste and see that the Lord is good through who I am. His mercy endures forever and He is my victory. The hand of the enemy is pushed back and God reigns and rules supreme over my life; spirit, soul and body. This is the day that the Lord has made, I will rejoice and will be glad in it!

Day Thirty

RAISED FROM THE DEAD

"After the Sabbath, at dawn on the first day of the week, Mary Magdalene and the other Mary went to look at the tomb. There was a violent earthquake, for an angel of the Lord came down from heaven and, going to the tomb, rolled back the stone and sat on it. His appearance was like lightning, and his clothes were white as snow. The guards were so afraid of him that they shook and became like dead men.

The angel said to the women, "Do not be afraid, for I know that you are looking for Jesus, who was crucified. He is not here; he has risen, just as he said. Come and see the place where he lay. Then go quickly and tell his disciples: 'He has risen from the dead and is going ahead of you into Galilee. There you will see him.' Now I have told you."

So the women hurried away from the tomb, afraid yet filled with joy, and ran to tell his disciples. Suddenly Jesus met them. "Greetings," he said. They came to him, clasped his feet and worshiped him. Then Jesus said to them, "Do not be afraid. Go and tell my brothers to go to Galilee; there they will see me."

Matthew 28:1-10

The whole of Christianity rises or falls on the reality of the resurrection. It was on the cross that Jesus suffered, died and became the only sacrifice acceptable to God on behalf of the sins of man. However, it was at this lonely tomb that the price that the price of Golgotha was validated. Had Jesus not risen from the dead, He simply would have been another religious guru that happened to have died on a cross. It was at this lonely hillside tomb, outside the city of Jerusalem that Jesus conquered death, hell and the grave by virtue of the power of resurrection.

The disciples have been on a three-year, whirlwind journey, with the world's most amazing man. It has taken them from a simple Jewish lifestyle to potential world-changers. They have watched this man perform astounding miracles. They saw him multiply food, walk on water, heal those that were sick, lame and blind. They even saw him raise the dead! They participated in the miracles themselves and their lives would never be the same.

Now, it has all come crashing down. The unimaginable has occurred and they stand empty, confused, and not quite sure of the future. Jesus is not only dead, but He died one of the worst deaths known to man. He died as a common criminal. The disciples not only had to endure His death, but also witnessed the shock, horror and brutality of a crucifixion. This couldn't be happening. Just weeks earlier, life was amazing and now, it seems that it was all just a dream that has become a nightmare.

In the hours following the brutal death of their friend, the disciples have somewhat of a memory of Jesus talking about a temple being destroyed and being raised up three days later, but what could that possibly mean? There was something He told them about having to "suffer at the hands of the elders, that he would be killed and raised back to life" (Matthew 16:21). It all seemed unclear now and none of it really made sense.

In their grieving, the ladies go to the tomb where they could mourn, talk about Jesus and about better times. To their amazement, the stone that sealed the tomb had been rolled back, an angel was sitting on the stone and declared to them that Jesus had risen from the dead even as He said. The angel was clear with his instructions to run and tell the disciples what they had seen and that Jesus was alive! On their way back to Galilee, Jesus,

Himself met the two women and showed Himself alive. This was a game changer and nothing would ever be the same!

Lessons of Victory

Hope and Life Restored! Four thousand years had passed from the time of Adam to Jesus. Under the heavy hand of demonic control, all of creation cried out for deliverance. Mankind needed a savior. The prophets decreed it, the people anticipated it and all of eternity depended on this one moment when Jesus rose from the dead. His earthly body lay in the tomb for three days, empty, deserted and nothing but a shell that once held the spirit of God, Himself. Death took Him, but death couldn't hold Him. With full life and authority, Jesus reclaimed what had been taken from Him. As He stepped back into His body by the power of resurrection, death, hell and the grave were defeated for all of eternity. He not only reclaimed His rightful place in both heaven and the earth, but also brought hope for millions of souls that would have been under the bondage of darkness.

I Am Forgiven. That is such a simple statement, but carries the weight of all eternity. The weight of sin affects everything about a person. The dark grip of sin creates a bondage that changes how you live, your perspective of life and even your worldview. Through the smog of sin, it is difficult to even begin to believe that you can be free. The resurrection changed that. Jesus made a way available for you and I to walk in the power of resurrection for ourselves, and to live victoriously over the lies and strategies of the enemy. Often, when contemplating the forgiveness of sin, we consider the cross, but without the resurrection, the cross would have been a moot point. Thank God for both!

Death is not the End. Once and for all, Jesus conquered the

186

grave. The resurrection is the divine promise of God that we too can live eternally. For the believer, death becomes nothing more than a gateway to being forever resurrected. Because of Jesus, we have gained entrance into the glories of heaven and the wonders of God. Paul lifts up his voice with authority and shouts, "Where, O death, is your victory? Where, O death, is your sting?" (1 Corinthians 15:55).

TODAY'S CONFESSION OF VICTORY

By the power of the resurrection, I am saved, I am healed, I am delivered, I am free! I am guaranteed an eternity of life with my Father in the realms of His love and wonder. I will not allow the lies and the strategies of the enemy to ensnare me and separate me from the resurrection power that is available to me through Jesus. That which was impossible has been conquered, opening the door for the miraculous to be evident in my life. I can live, I can serve, I can be all that God has called me to be. I have the power to overcome sin, and to have a dynamic relationship with Jesus Christ. I walk in joy, confidence and the authority that is mine through the resurrection.

Day Thirty One

IN ONE ACCORD

"When the Day of Pentecost had fully come, they were all with one accord in one place. And suddenly there came a sound from heaven, as of a rushing mighty wind, and it filled the whole house where they were sitting. Then there appeared to them divided tongues, as of fire, and one sat upon each of them. And they were all filled with the Holy Spirit and began to speak with other tongues, as the Spirit gave them utterance."

Acts 2:1-4

By now, the disciples of Jesus are used to lives that were anything but ordinary. For the last three years, Jesus has introduced them to a way of living that they never could have even begun to imagine. Through the life of Jesus, heaven invaded earth and these disciples were caught up in the excitement and thrill of all that being with the Messiah meant. They saw and heard the miraculous on a regular basis and experienced the great joys of seeing broken bodies restored, those in bondage set free and the kingdom of God established in power and righteousness.

At the end of three years, they walked through the worst tragedy imaginable. Jesus has been brutally crucified and all of their hopes and dreams have been shattered. Then came the miracle. As promised, Jesus rose from the dead and showed Himself alive to the disciples as well as many others. During the forty days following the resurrection, Jesus gave specific instructions for the disciples to gather in Jerusalem and to "wait for the promise of the Father" (Acts 1:4).

Gathered together in an "upper room", they sought the Lord, worshipped and waited. In response to their passion and commitment to follow the Lord, the Holy Spirit came into the room as a rushing mighty wind and with flames of fire and each of them were endued with power from heaven. The torch has been passed. Salvation for mankind has been secured, the kingdom of God has been reestablished on the earth and these fledgling leaders have been empowered to preach this new gospel to the ends of the earth. Life would never be the same. The world would never be the same. Millions of people from that day forward would never be the same. God's rule has been secured and just as He chose to use two humans in the garden of Eden to rule and reign on the earth with Him, He has now raised up a new generation that will spread the good news throughout the earth!

Lessons of Victory

<u>Unity opens the Door to the Miraculous.</u> The scripture makes it clear that these disciples "were all in one accord" (Acts 2:1). To fully understand the importance and implications of the word "accord", it's beneficial to break down the Greek word in order to glean the heart of God and discover why unity is such an important factor in accomplishing the great commission that Jesus gave. The original Greek word is "homothumadon". It's made up from two separate words; "Homou" which means to assemble yourselves together, and "thumos" which means to possess a fierce passion.

To further understand the implications of "thumos", we must take a look at its word origin, which is "thuo". "Thuo" is derived from the context of sacrificing the paschal lamb. Jesus was the paschal lamb of God, slain before the foundation of the world (Revelation 13:8). His death and resurrection ignited a deep and fierce passion in the hearts of the disciples that would never be quenched. They were willing to lay down their very lives for the sake of the gospel, and many of them did. The unity that these early believers experienced was a deeply moving conviction of what Jesus had accomplished in their lives and on their behalf. That an innocent man and the Son of God would willingly give His life for them was a compelling factor that had changed them forever. They weren't in this upper room hiding or trying to figure out all that had just occurred! They were waiting on orders. They were passionate, purposeful and carrying a heavenly mandate.

Being in "one accord" brings clarity of heart and mind. Unity at this level actually serves as a deterrent to the strategies and lies of the enemy that would seek to undermine the purposes of God. It is through unity that God manifests His power and authority on the earth as the power of agreement activates the anointing and accelerates the miraculous.

Get Ready for the Suddenly Moments of God! God is in the suddenly business! Throughout the scriptures, we find Him moving suddenly in people's lives, often when they least expected it. Moses found himself on the backside of the desert when "suddenly" he encountered the living God in a burning bush. Mary was minding her own business, planning a wedding when "suddenly" she was visited by an archangel and her life was radically changed forever by the news that she would give birth to the Messiah. These disciples were having a wonderful prayer meeting when "suddenly" they were filled with the power of the Holy Spirit.

Actually, the suddenly moments of God aren't suddenly at all. They are part of a divinely orchestrated plan that arrived at the right season of your life and was designed by God to advance you to the next level. Life with the Father is always an amazing adventure. He is full of surprises and delights in lavishing His love and kingdom moments upon His children. When we take the time to draw closer to Him and fully follow His promptings and His heart, awesome things are bound to happen. Our place is one of complete dependence and obedience upon the Lord. When we submit ourselves to Him, we open the door for the suddenly moments and the life-changing experiences that can come only from Him.

What you Hear always precedes what you See. There are "sounds of heaven" that wash over the earth, but can only be heard by the discerning ear. The sound of heaven is sometimes that of a "rushing mighty wind" (Acts 2:2) and sometimes that of a still small voice (1 Kings 19:12). It has been accurately stated that "you must say what you hear, to see what you said". The prophetic whisper of God is released prior to the manifestations of God. "Surely the Lord God does nothing, Unless He reveals His secret to His servants the prophets" (Amos 3:7). That revelation is the sound of heaven. Upon that revelation, the prophetic utterance is decreed and God's responds with supernatural visitation as He did in the upper room. It is imperative that you spend time listening for the sound of heaven. Hearing the sweet voice of Holy Spirit brings revelation, nourishment, correction and vision to your heart.

Life in the Power of the Holy Spirit. God poured out His Spirit in an amazing way for the purposes of strengthening and advancing the kingdom. The fresh wind of the Holy Spirit is blowing across the world today as the Body of Christ is rising up to a new place of revelation, passion and commitment to fulfill the great commission. The gifts of the Spirit are becoming the standard once again in those that are hungry for a real move of God. The people of God are being revitalized as fresh fire is falling from heaven and the anointing of life and ministry is increasing. These are the days of great outpouring and a great in-gathering of the harvest. Hearts that have grown cold are being restored to the passion and love that they once held. Churches that have become weak and ineffective are rising up with fire in their gatherings and communities that have been paralyzed with satanic lies and bondages are being set free by those that are walking in the power of this new era. These are the greatest days of the kingdom of God and the power of the Holy Spirit is being released in a new and fresh way!

TODAY'S CONFESSION OF VICTORY

Fill me, Lord! I am ready for the fullness of Your Spirit in my life. I open my heart to all that You have for me and I willingly submit to Your purposes and plans for my life. I prophesy that the power and the anointing of Holy Spirit overflows in every area of my life. I stand in awe at Your greatness and bask in the magnitude of Your love for me. I am strong in You and I rise up today to take my place in the release of the kingdom across the earth today. I have been born for such a time as this and the magnitude of my calling demands that I am filled with the Holy Spirit.

Flow freely through me. May the gifts of the Spirit be evident in my life and in all that I do. May those that I encounter find the love, grace and healing that flows from Holy Spirit in my life and may it be poured out to theirs.

ABOUT THE AUTHOR

Scott Reece is a man who is passionate about the Word of God! With 40 years of ministry experience, he has served as a youth pastor, church planter, lead pastor and as a denominational district supervisor. Currently, Scott and his wife, Michelle serve as lead pastors of MGT New Hope Church in Moline, Illinois. Together, they lead a multi-cultural and generational congregation that is impacting a community, nation and world.

As a father of six children and as a grandfather, his passion is to see the next generation rise up and embrace the truth and authority of the Word of God and change the world through the power of the Word!

www.thefaithfactor.blogspot.com